Recipes for Good Living

The Beginner's Guide
to Spirituality

Recipes for Good Living

The Beginner's Guide to Spirituality

Terry Biddington

Illustrated by Fiona Biddington

Circle Books

Winchester, UK
Washington, USA

First published by O-Books, 2012
O-Books is an imprint of John Hunt Publishing Ltd., Laurel House, Station Approach,
Alresford, Hants, SO24 9JH, UK
office1@o-books.net
www.o-books.com

For distributor details and how to order please visit the 'Ordering' section on our website.

ISBN: 978 1 84694 902 9

A CIP catalogue record for this book is available from the British Library.

Design: Stuart Davies

Printed in the USA by Edwards Brothers Malloy

.

We operate a distinctive and ethical publishing philosophy in all
areas of our business, from our global network of authors to
production and worldwide distribution.

CONTENTS

Introduction

Welcome to the first day of the rest of your life!

So here you are – you may be away from your folks for the first time, living more or less independently with family and friends, or completely by yourself in the middle of hundreds of strangers in a new and entirely unfamiliar place.

You'll likely have more unsupervised activity and time on your hands than you've ever had before and the freedom to do exactly what you choose! For some of you, that's just what you've been looking forward to for ages! For others among you, it may be a really scary thought.

Ever since you can remember you've probably been looked after by other people. You've been told what to do, what not to wear, who not to watch, and what time to get home. You've had a regular daily routine, a school or college timetable, and someone to do your ironing. Now it's over to you big time – and no parents' evenings when they can check easily on your progress!

So where exactly do you begin? How can you do everything you want to do and still focus on your work? How will you find time to look after yourself, wash your underwear, and do all those necessary jobs others used to do for you – to say nothing of cooking?

These days, fewer and fewer people can cook or be bothered to prepare decent food for themselves. Not even soup. It's a basic fact of life. But there are some great books out there to start you off. Junk food is ok once or twice a week, but you can't survive on it for too long. "You are what you eat," someone once said, and to flourish you need to eat healthily. Most of the time, at least! You'll need to get some decent nourishment inside you and, as today is the first day of the rest of your life, you might as well start right now.

Why spirituality?

What you eat each day, just like what you do with your time and your money, what you wear and whether or not you exercise, is now entirely up to you. And you will need to think about each of these things, because they matter. In fact it's possible to say that all of these things are actually *spiritual* matters, because life is a spiritual matter!

Now spirituality is not the same as religion. Some people practice a religion – Christianity, Islam, Judaism, Hinduism, and so on. But all people have a "spiritual" dimension, even if they don't use that word.

Lifestyle

Having a spirituality is about having a lifestyle that tries to balance, integrate, and harmonize all the different aspects of who you are and how you lead your life: your daily routines, your mental and physical health, your social networks, the music you listen to, even right down to the coffee you drink and how much time you spend surfing the net and twittering.

Spirituality is also about your thoughts, feelings and values, and the people and things you care about, including your self-identity and sexuality. Spirituality is *lifestyle with attitude*. It matters! And you need to learn to nurture your own personal spirituality just as you do the rest of your experience of being alive.

Finding "soul food"

There is a theory that says it was in discovering how to cook – how fire could transform raw food into something more nourishing – that our ancestors took the final evolutionary step to becoming human. Be that as it may, it's certainly true that nurturing your soul – finding the things that best help you thrive – is a lot like learning how to cook. You'll need to find what Thomas Moore in his *Care of the Soul* calls the "recipes for good living"[1] that work for you and allow you to flourish. "Good food," he says, "is part of soulfulness."[2]

So while it's true that now you can do exactly what you like and try all sorts of new things, it stands to common sense that not everything is going to be right *for you* - even if you're not exactly sure who you are at the moment!

Discovering your spirituality

Your spirituality changes over time, just like who and what you are now isn't the same as it was even two years ago. Your spirituality changes in response to your developing identity, relationships, and experience of life. *So are you interested in setting out on a journey of exploration to find out more about yourself?*

Try this recipe

- Begin by making a few bullet points outlining your thoughts about this journey.
- What do you hope to discover?
- What are your fears?
- Where would you like to arrive at your journey's end?
- What sort of person would you like to have become?

Getting Started

A great way to get started is to make a list of the things that are important to you. The things you need in your life and that make you tick. While it can be as detailed as you like, you may find it better to make bullet points. Either way your list will probably contain at least some of the following:

1   The stuff that's "been given" to you that you can't do much about. Your family and background; where you're coming from. You may really wish lots of this were different than it is – and may even pretend your experience *is* different –

but it's there in your past and you have to work through it, as we'll see later. Try listing all the key moments and "givens" in your life so far.

2 Your preferences in music, clothes, food, film, sport, hobbies, and so on. Stick to some main categories.

3 Your experience of relationships with your family and friends, your desires and fantasies, your feelings about your gender and sexuality. How you feel about your body and the way you look. Loads of important stuff here that we'll come back to.

4 Your daily routines. What are those perfectly ordinary little things that matter to you every day? Tea or coffee in the morning? Breakfast? Shower or bath? Brisk early jog or last minute rush? What is it that you need to make your day complete?

5 Your favorite places to be to unwind and chill. Long walks or logs fires? The beach in summer or a winter storm? The countryside or a football terrace? In the silence of a church and sacred space – or the excitement and noise of a club or pub? By yourself or with others?

6 Your values. What are the personal qualities you have that are important to you? Friendliness and approachability? Loyalty? Courage? Honesty? Sense of humor? Being up for risks and adventures – or preferring tried and tested ways?

7 Your views on the issues that are important to you: world peace and justice, the environment, politics, religion, why it is you're veggie – or not. There are lots of issues here, but don't worry if you haven't thought all of the details through. That's normal; but you'll already have a good idea of the things that concern you.

8 Your hopes and aspirations for the future. And don't worry if you're not at all sure what these are. It'll become clearer as you go on.

Be honest with yourself!

At this point your list may look a bit like the outline of a personal advert in the dating pages of a newspaper! But this stuff is for your own private benefit – so you need to be honest with yourself or else the task of discovering your spirituality will be impossible.

You'll probably know all about coping with peer group pressure. And you'll be something of an expert in walking the line between wanting to be part of the group and being your own person. It can often be so difficult to be different from the crowd! But the reality is that no-one is perfect. And part of being a fully-rounded person is knowing and recognizing this. An awareness and acceptance of who you really are – warts and all – is an important part of discovering and valuing your spirituality.

Walking on the dark side

And then there's what is often called your "shadow" side: that bit of your personality that you keep under wraps from everyone, that side of you that few if any see. Everyone has one and it's different in everyone, but one of the things we all need to do is to try to explore and understand this part of ourselves. It can be hard work! And while it'll always be part of you – getting to understand it will help you to appreciate who you are and why you think, behave, and react in certain ways.

Making connections

But discovering your spirituality isn't just about you! As you become more aware of yourself as a spiritual being – of who you really are and what makes you tick – you will begin to make connections with other people and the world around you. You will become more aware of the pain and suffering in the world. You will start to feel yourself intimately connected to the rest of the global family, with the whole of creation and, in a strange way, with the unfolding mystery of the universe itself.

Becoming fully human

Centuries ago a guy called Irenaeus wrote that "the glory of God is a human being who is fully alive."[3] Now don't be put off by the "G-Word." Whether or not you believe in God, the idea of being *fully human* is a fascinating one. What does it mean? Does it mean having everything we want in life – wealth, riches, and fame – in order to ensure our own personal flourishing? Does it mean that we should try to understand everything about ourselves and the human condition? Does it involve us in exploring how we can be individuals within a complex interdependent network with the rest of humanity? And does it further mean that if we are to nurture and value ourselves, we can only do so if we also ensure that everyone else – and the whole planet – is also nurtured and valued?

Let's summarize what we've said so far:

- Everyone has a spiritual dimension – and for every one it's different.
- Our spirituality is something to be explored; it changes, grows, and unfolds throughout our life time.
- It may be likened to a collage of thoughts, beliefs, experiences, memories, and practices.
- It can be expressed in a million ways – and for some people it involves practicing a particular religion.
- Learning what is spiritual for us is an important part of living as a human being.
- Spirituality is both "special" and "ordinary." Just like life itself!
- Understanding our own spirituality helps us to have an awareness of the needs and lives, the pain and joy of others. It has a practical dimension.
- We can better nurture our spiritual self when we see ourselves as part of the one human family, mutually interdependent with our global environment.

7

Up for an adventure?

Are you wondering how to find out more about your spirituality right now? It's quite a roller-coaster ride – but here goes!

Try this Simple Quiz

(to get a sense of what your spirituality might look like)

For each question choose the answer that occurs to you first.

1 You see a glorious sunset. What do you do?
   a Stand there in awe
   b Go inside and watch TV
   c Take a photo

2 What's more important to you?
   a Getting a good degree
   b Living a full life
   c Earning lots of money

3 Happiness is ...?
   a Being content
   b Having another drink
   c Discovering who I am and who I'm meant to be

4 The spiritual life is all about:
   a Going regularly to church/mosque/synagogue/etc
   b Changing the world
   c Living as responsibly and creatively as possible

5 What is your motto in life?
   a Live long and prosper
   b Eat, drink, and be merry: for tomorrow we die
   c It's better to travel than to arrive

6 What would you like to see written on your tombstone?
    a I told you I was ill
    b I hope I did little harm to others
    c Thank you

7 A good work of art:
    a Grabs the soul
    b Is worth a fortune
    c Should mean something

8 Life is all about:
    a Making the best of it we can
    b Being responsible for my own actions
    c Never doing anything wrong

9 What's more important to you?
    a Feeding people
    b Converting people to your way of seeing the world
    c Helping to make a difference

10 Good relationships are all about:
    a The joy of discovering other people
    b Learning to give and take
    c Getting other people to like me

11 Silence leaves me feeling:
    a Bored
    b Restored and re-energized
    c Connected to the universe

12 A good night out means:
    a Getting drunk
    b Being with friends
    c Just spending money

13 What do you enjoy most?
    a   Sitting quietly
    b   Being in a crowded room
    c   A walk in the countryside

14 Crying is:
    a   A sign of vulnerability
    b   A sign of my humanity
    c   A sign I need to see a counselor

15 I feel connected to the universe:
    a   At a football match
    b   In a pub, bar, or club
    c   On a seashore or in a park

16 My idea of relaxation is:
    a   A long soak in the bath
    b   Watching a good film
    c   A five-mile jog

17 Laughter is:
    a   Important to me
    b   The best medicine
    c   A gift for sharing

18 What do you most want out of life?
    a   Fame and fortune
    b   A peaceful death at a very old age
    c   The chance to make a difference

19 Listening to music or watching a film
    a   Helps me chill
    b   Makes me feel great
    c   Stops me feeling bored

20 Which of these would you say?
    a   I have a body
    b   I am a body
    c   I wish I had a different body

Scores:

1. a) 4	b) 0	c) 4	11. a) 0 b) 4	c) 4
2. a) 4	b) 4	c) 2	12. a) 0 b) 4	c) 0
3. a) 4	b) 0	c) 4	13. a) 4 b) 4	c) 4
4. a) 2	b) 3	c) 4	14. a) 3 b) 4	c) 2
5. a) 4	b) 3	c) 4	15. a) 4 b) 4	c) 4
6. a) 4	b) 4	c) 4	16 a) 4 b) 4	c) 4
7. a) 4	b) 2	c) 3	17 a) 4 b) 4	c) 4
8. a) 3	b) 4	c) 0	18 a) 2 b) 3	c) 4
9. a) 4	b) 2	c) 4	19 a) 4 b) 4	c) 2
10. a) 3	b) 4	c) 2	20 a) 4 b) 4	c) 3

So how did you do?
40-60?   A good place to start from!
61-77?   You've got what it takes!!
78+?   Clearly a very spiritual type!!!

Feel free to try it again by yourself!
You make now like to give your own responses to the following statements. This will help you to build up a more authentic sketch of your own spirituality at this initial stage of your journey.

Remember, no one else will see this. So you can be completely honest with yourself.

1   *You see a glorious sunset.*
    What do you do?
    Why?
2   *What's really most important to you at this stage of your life?*

Why?

3 *What makes you really happy?*
Why?

4 *What do find spiritual about life?*
Why?

5 *What do you enjoy about life?*
Why?

6 *How would you like to be remembered?*
Why?

7 *Good relationships are all about?*
What?
Why?

8 *Silence leaves you feeling?*
Why?

9 *What do you most enjoy doing?*
Why?

10 *What makes you feel connected to the universe?*
Why?

11 *What do you most want out of life?*
Why?

12 *What do you like or dislike about your body?*
Why?

No wrong answers

Needless to say, this time there are no scores. Whatever you've written is the right answer for you!

There'll be another opportunity to do this exercise again later on. But for now you may like to spend some time by yourself – or with someone you trust – thinking about what you've said about yourself.

And well done for being so honest!

Setting Out On the Journey

It's time now to set off on your further adventures and explorations!

You'll see that the basic idea of this book is that, because your spirituality has an infinitely variable number of ingredients, it's rather like trying out different recipes in a cookbook and then, if they work, making them part of your favorite "spiritual menu."

Food and cooking have often been used to talk about the mystery of human spiritual development.

As any cook or chef will tell you, there are some important and essential techniques that need to be mastered until you eventually get the hang of them. And it's just the same with the spiritual life. There are some techniques, some spiritual recipes if you like, which are basic essentials and can't be ditched if you fail at the first attempt.

Like with so much else in life, there's no substitute for patient and determined hard work, practice, and effort. The more you put in, the more you get out!

So let's have a look at those essential ingredients to a fulfilling spiritual life.

A FeW INgredIENTS

The Essentials

What follows is an introduction to five key essentials. They need to be studied carefully as they form the basic kit for starting off on your own and discovering how to flourish.

There are five chapters. *"Spirituality and personality"* and *"Taste and see"* encourage us to see ourselves as individuals with our own particular spiritual needs. Next comes *"Free food"* where we discover that there really can be something for nothing, if we know how to find it. Then *"Making bread"* shows us how to make things last and go further, how to sustain ourselves spiritually The fifth and final essential is *"Beware. Death in the pot!"* which looks at what to do when the recipe goes wrong and things turn sour.

The rest of the book, the *Recipe Section,* can be read methodically from end to end, or dipped into as the fancy takes you.

What's important to remember is that, like any cookery book, what follows is mostly meant to be a practical manual for things to be *tried out and practiced.* So you'll need to be:

- up for having a go
- open-minded about the outcomes
- not put off if you don't "succeed" first time
- committed to finding out more about yourself
- willing to explore what "life in all its fullness" – and in all its consequences – might be for you

Top tip
You will probably find it really useful to buy a notebook to write down all your observations and reflections.

Essential 1: Spirituality and Personality

People everywhere are waking up to the fact that, because we all have different personalities – personality types – this will affect the way we are as spiritual people. You can buy books on the subject, but here is a place to start thinking.

Are you an introvert or an extrovert?

People are either basically "introvert" or "extrovert." Now while these terms are quite commonly used in day to day language – where "introvert" is sometimes used in a derogatory sense and "extrovert" often sounds more interesting – they have a more specific meaning for us. Here *both terms are equal in value* and we can briefly define them as follows.

Extroverts

Extroverts are people who get their spiritual energy, their spiritual "fix":

- from things outside of themselves
- from other people

- from interacting with the world
- from standing before the awesome natural world

Or else extroverts may be energized by using objects – often called "symbols" or "totems" – to help them focus or access their spiritual dimension:

- incense and candles
- stones, crosses, beads
- images, mandalas, icons
- Extroverts like variety and action.

Introverts

Introverts are people who get in touch with their spiritual side:

- from inside of themselves
- by closing their eyes to the world and entering the "darkness"
- by "centering themselves" in the stillness
- by going deep down inside to reach their spiritual "heart," "center," or "wellspring"
- Introverts like quiet and stillness for concentration.

Nothing is fixed forever

While both extroverts and introverts have an innate, natural preference to be as they are (and though they can gradually change over time), it's vital to remember that a great deal can be learned by exploring the "other" side. So extroverts can explore their introvert side or dimension, and introverts their extrovert side or dimension. This "swapping" can be hard work – exhausting and sometimes quite painful – but it can also produce amazing results in terms of a deeper self-understanding and a more integrated spirituality.

What's really important to remember, though, is for the most part it's vital to be the person you are now, as honestly or "authentically" as you can!

What is your own experience?

If you're unsure whether you're an extrovert or an introvert try these two simple exercises.

1 Talk to as many people as you can in thirty minutes. Listen carefully to what they say. Interact with them as much as you can.

2 Go and sit somewhere quiet by yourself with your eyes closed for ten minutes. Try not to be distracted by the things around you or to think too much about anything. Just concentrate on breathing slowly.

How does that make you feel?

Which of the two exercises made you feel more energized? Which one left you feeling more in touch with yourself? Which did you prefer – and why do you think that was?

Try these recipes

- Practice these exercises on a daily basis for a while and see what happens.
- Find out what resources are out there on the internet, or freely available from nature, to help you get in touch with your spiritual side.

Essential 2: Taste and See

Trying things out

It's important to realize that, because everyone is different, whether you're "introvert" or "extrovert," there will be a great many possible approaches to developing your spirituality. What's important is to find what works for you. Remember that your spirituality or daily spiritual practice is like a "collage" or "montage" of things that are unique to you, like a feast of your own devising. As you try new things out some of them won't work for you and some will. And the things that do work for you will become part of the "mixture" that is your spiritual practice or discipline.

In some sense creating your own spiritual discipline can be like choosing what to eat from a menu or helping yourself from a buffet or "smorgas board" laden with different dishes. Or indeed like shopping in a "spiritual supermarket" or choosing a new novel from library shelves full of authors' names you've never heard of. The only way to proceed is to "taste and see" what you prefer!

Some contemporary religious writers claim this "DIY" approach demeans the very idea of spirituality. They use words like "hodgepodge" and "pick and mix" to somehow suggest a spirituality that is "cheap and nasty," "hopelessly jumbled," "confused," and therefore "low grade," "impure," and "not quite the real thing."

Not just the sweet course!
If we continue the analogy with the buffet or smorgas board, however, it becomes clear that, because we can choose whatever we like, we may find ourselves holding a plate made up entirely of one sort of food. We may indulge ourselves by just eating the sweet stuff.

While this may be a pleasant indulgence as a "one-off," we all recognize that, to nourish ourselves properly, we need to eat a range of food: protein, carbohydrate, and roughage, as well as some sweet things. And that's what most of us do most of the time. We usually recognize the need to have a balanced diet.

Send for the "food doctor?"
Now there has long been a tendency for some people to set themselves up as "experts": people who "know what's best for us" and who are happy to tell us what to do. And, this shouldn't surprise us, because there is in most of us a part of our psyche that is precisely all about needing to be told what to do and what's best for us!

Perhaps it's because we are "busy people," just plain lazy, or simply can't face up to life's challenges in a mature way, that too few of us seem to want to take responsibility for our own spiritual health! So we seek out gurus, spiritual guides, and teachers or look around for help: for time-saving shortcuts, for "top tips" and "win-win" strategies to make it that much easier.

Costing an arm and a leg?
Some of the spiritual advice that's readily available comes with a pretty hefty price tag. And it's so easy to spend money if we convince ourselves that the latest handbook or manual will

effortlessly change our lives! Indeed I was once approached at a
"Mind, Body, Spirit Fair" by someone offering to help me "make
real money out of spiritual need." I could, they suggested, easily
become a spiritual guru on the internet, take advantage of
people's need, and "make money even when you're not on-line!"

As a general rule, we must beware those who offer spiritual
guidance in return for money. For there's a lot of great advice
readily available and quite free of charge if you know where to
look, as we'll discover later.

So what can you "taste and see" to discover how to be more
in tune with your spiritual side?

Whether you're "introvert" or "extrovert," you may like to
begin by trying some of the following:

- Keep some special or "sacred" object on your desk, in your
  room, at your place of work, or on your person. It may be
  something that will speak to you and remind you of your
  deeper self and your connectedness to the "bigger
  picture," and the world around you: symbols, images,
  texts, and quotations. Anything that has this significance
  for you.
- Begin each day with a sense of thankfulness simply for
  being alive in the "here and now," and with openness and
  anticipation to all that a new day will bring. Every day is
  unique and never-to-be-repeated. How will you choose to
  spend it?

Spend five minutes everyday looking at the world and finding
something of beauty in it. You never have to look far to find
something to take your breath away. Learn to see the most
mundane and common things as unique works of art and beauty.

- Learn to live with your imperfections: for no-one is
  perfect. Be gentle with yourself. It's usually the best way to

remedy or address the things you would like to change about yourself.

- Deal with others as you would have them deal with you, and try to be more tolerant of their shortcomings. Someone once said that we dislike the people we do, because they actually remind us of the things we dislike in ourselves. That's worth thinking about!
- Look for meaning and purpose in the work that you do. It's generally there, just beneath the surface. Find the ways in which what you're doing links you to the wider world. Keep making the connections and let this skill become part of your spiritual discipline. It's so important to think and act "outside the box": creatively and with imagination
- Try to do one thing each day to connect you to the global human family. At the very least make sure you catch up with the world news.
- Spend five minutes at the end of your day looking back over it. Don't *judge* what you did – just note how you experienced and reacted to the various events.

Take time each day to be open to the unfolding of your spirituality!

Try these recipes

If you have "extrovert" tendencies:

- Go and sit in a crowded place and notice the people around you. See how different they are. Imagine what their stories might be. Try to notice the spiritual in each of them.
- Talk to someone who looks in need of conversation.
- Find a place to volunteer that will bring you into contact with other people.

If you have "introvert" tendencies:

- Find space alone to recharge your batteries; take ten or fifteen minutes to be absolutely still and silent.
- Think of a phrase or quotation that you like – and repeat it slowly to yourself.
- Learn to "center down." Imagine that you are going deep down inside yourself (or else rising high above yourself) and making contact with your very essence, that small point of light at your very heart. Stay there for as long as you can and be open to what you find.
- Go for a slow walk by yourself. Notice things and people. Find a place to stop and just be.

Whatever your experience

Whether you're "extrovert" or "introvert," you will probably find it helpful to:

- Make sure to keep a note of what you feel and experience.
- Join a group or activity that suits your spirituality.
- Get involved in the struggles for justice of people other than yourself.
- Try to explore some of the things suggested for your "shadow" or "opposite" side.

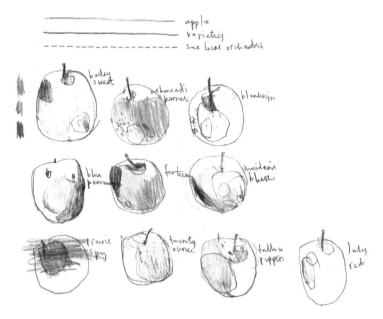

Essential 3: Finding Free Food

As part of the wide scale movement to rediscover the delights of "growing your own" fruit and vegetables and the upsurge in demand for allotments, many cities and towns have begun to search for unused space to offer people. These include disused plots, abandoned sports fields, roadside verges, and those odd bits of land that no-one has ever quite known what to do with.

People have also been encouraged to offer their gardens for others to grow things, or themselves as free labor in return for a share of the harvest. Many local authorities and town councils have also undertaken to plant fruit trees in public places and to map the existing ones so that people can help themselves to fruit that would otherwise go to waste. The results are amazing, and thousands of fruit trees and patches of wild fruit of all sorts have been discovered. To find out what's available in your area, visit your local council's website.

While these are really creative and exciting developments in themselves, they also highlight an important point about life itself: its gratuitousness!

Life's a gift

Now this may not be a word that's familiar to you, so here's the back story. There used to be a time when the post woman or mailman, dustmen or garbage collectors, or paper boys and girls would knock at your door just before Christmas and smile meaningfully at you. They were after their annual bonus or tip. Their gratuity.

If you've ever worked in a bar or restaurant you'll know all about tips and gratuities, while the rest of us will have often been faced with the dilemma of whether or not to offer one! Do we tip for good service or because we like the look of the person who's served us? Do they have to have done something to merit the bonus? Or do we give it just for the hell of it – *the joy of it* – whether or not they have done anything to deserve it?

The point I think it's important for us to catch is that *life itself is gratuitous.* Just like those fruit trees and bushes whose seeds germinate and grow, and keep on blossoming and fruiting, so life itself is given to us "for nothing." We didn't ask to be born – how could we? – and yet, ever since our birth day, life itself has been there for us. Sure, there are times when life can be sheer torture, and when we could do without some of its trials and tribulations: but life just keeps being poured out for us. Every day a fresh start, a new beginning, a new birth, even. Every day is a new day for us to use as we choose.

Saying "Yes" to life

Now at first glance, perhaps, this may seem an incurably romantic view, hopelessly optimistic, and willfully – wickedly? – ignoring all the pain and suffering that's out there! But the only cure or antidote for the riskiness involved in living life to the full is to learn to say "Yes" to life itself; to all of it, "warts and all."

Living life day by day, season by season, is all about being open to making new and exciting discoveries. Unanticipated fruit trees around every corner, unexpected new things, ideas, relationships, unbidden insights, and astonishing moments of "grace": magical moments when we feel strangely and unconditionally happy, loved, valued, or blessed.

Yes. The best things in life are indeed free! But it sounds a bit too good to be true. So what's the catch?

There is one: and it's this. Life is a terminal condition. We will all die one day. And all we can do is to learn to love life *precisely because* it is the way it is.

What is your own experience?

- When was the last time you did something completely gratuitously, for yourself or another person – for the sheer joy of doing it?
- What discoveries have you already made about yourself since you began this journey of exploration?

Try these recipes

- Make a list of all the good things in your life that you have received for nothing.
- What do you have to give away to help nourish other people?

Essential 4: Making Bread

There are those people who say that making their own bread is simply not worth the trouble.

"Why go to all that effort," they say, "when there are so many sorts of bread readily available at the shop around the corner or on the next block?" That's true, of course. But it doesn't mean they're not missing a trick. There's something exciting and creative about making bread. It's like getting in touch with a primitive and visceral part of what it means to be human.

You begin by taking some of the basic elements of life that people have used for countless millennia: grain, yeast, salt, oil, and water. You may also want to add secret extra ingredients according to your particular taste: herbs, honey, spices of various kinds. Then you mix them all together.

The mixing together – kneading – is the fun part. Turning the dough in upon itself, over and over, massaging it, stretching it, and then folding it back upon itself again. The point is not only to blend the ingredients together, but to let the air into the mix, without which the dough won't work. After the kneading it needs time to rise in a warm place and then heat or fire to bake it. Believe me, there's nothing on earth quite so amazing as that first taste of your newly baked bread!

It may come as a surprise to discover that the idea of kneading dough and making bread has long been used in the Jewish religion as a metaphor for studying scripture. You take the holy text – containing everything you believe is "essential to leading a good life" – and then you "turn it and turn it," looking at it from every side and interrogating it energetically, just as you'd knead the dough. You let it simmer and rise in your mind and then share the nourishment with others to enjoy.

Bread of life

But you might also like to consider that the idea of bread making is also a good way to describe the process of working out what's going on with your own life. What are the essential ingredients of your life? What is the basic water and grain that has been given you by your birth and upbringing? What is the special yeast that you've learned gives your life its energy, spirit, and dynamism? What have you discovered gives it salt, spice, and zest? What oils do you use when the going gets tough and you need to be gentle with yourself and with others? Do you let life stretch you in exciting new directions? And do you give yourself enough time and space to rise and become the person you're meant to be?

Bread making is all about taking life's essential raw ingredients and transforming them into something even more nutritious and sustaining. The same is true about discovering your spirituality when you sit down to chew over the ordinary things of your life and wonder how they might be transformed, so that you can become whatever you need to be in order to thrive and flourish and bring a blessing for others.

Kneading dough is hard work and takes effort and patience if you want to have good bread to share.

So too the spiritual life! If you don't want to end up with something synthetic and tasteless, you need to accept that the process of nurturing your own spirituality is essentially organic. It requires honesty, authenticity, and commitment. In particular it needs you to be ready to be tougher with yourself when things seem too effortless and also gentler with yourself when the going gets tough! In this way you will open yourself up enough to let yourself breathe and so allow the spirit within you to work.

When the bread goes stale

Good bread and good spirituality are key ingredients to ensuring our own sustainability. But, despite our best intentions, sometimes the bread goes stale. And generally this happens when we are most in need of nourishment!

Stale bread is usually thrown away. It has very few uses unless it is refreshed by being allowed to soak up or absorb the new moisture or flavor that comes with a different recipe. And it's the same with our spiritual self. For when our spiritual life becomes stale and musty with over familiar routines, practices, and assumptions, we need the reinvigorating energy that comes when new moisture, savor, or zest is added. And this happens when we discover a new formula for living.

Seek the mystery ingredients

While there are some very good tried-and-tested recipes in this spiritual cookery book, and in the great religions of the world, there is no "ready-made" remedy that can be given that doesn't require at least some hard work on your part. For each of us is unique with different needs. We have to find what works for us and keeps us "fresh" and vibrant.

The secret is that freshness and vibrancy come with being ever open to the things that give us real sustenance and energy, and that keep us creative, compassionate, and spiritually healthy. These are the things that will keep us going and thriving as we set off on our journey.

What is your own experience?
- What are the essential ingredients of your own life?
- Which of these ingredients is absolutely indispensable – and what could you discard?
- Are there ways in which you feel you need to grow as an individual?

- What's your experience of life going stale? What did you do about it?

Try these recipes

- Make a list of the things that give you creative energy and open you up to new possibilities.
- In what ways might you need to begin to stretch your mental and spiritual horizons?
- Try this simple recipe to make yourself some bread. Use the time you spend kneading the dough to meditate on your own life.

Take 225g (7.8 oz) strong white flour and 225g granary bread flour and mix in a large bowl. Add one teaspoon of salt, one of caster sugar, and about 7 grams/a 2.5 oz sachet of easy-blend yeast. With your fist, make a hole in the flour and pour in 150 ml (.25 pint) of warm milk, one beaten egg, and a table spoon of olive oil. Little by little, add warm (but not hot) water until you've made a wet, soft dough that sticks to your fingers.

On a lightly floured table or flat surface, knead the dough for ten minutes. Really work it! Then put it back in the bowl, cover it with a clean damp cloth, and leave it in a warm place until it doubles in size.

At this point cut the dough into shapes for rolls and place them on floured or buttered baking sheets. If you want loaves break off enough dough to half fill a bread tin. Leave everything for a further thirty minutes until it's doubled in size again.

If you're making rolls, heat the oven to gas mark 6/180 C. With a pastry brush (or clean finger!), rub a little egg yolk on the top of each roll and bake for 15-20 minutes until they look golden brown and sufficiently risen. If you're making loaves, heat the oven to gas mark 5/170 C. Brush with the egg yolk and bake for 45-50 minutes (or about 20 minutes for smaller loaves) until they look interesting.

Then take out your bread and leave it to cool for as long as you can resist the temptation! Then eat it slowly and remember to congratulate yourself.

Essential 5: Beware. Death in the Pot!

There's a great story in the Jewish scriptures about a dinner party that goes dreadfully wrong. (See 2 Kings, chapter 4.)

When important visitors arrive a stew is prepared with a selection of randomly gathered wild gourds – pumpkins, squashes, marrows, cucumbers, and so on. The ingredients are diced, seasoned with herbs, hastily stirred into a large cooking pot, and set to simmer while the drinks are poured. A tasty veggie improvisation is keenly anticipated by the proud chef!

In due course the guests are served and they tuck in eagerly. However, they have hardly swallowed their first mouthfuls when they retch and splutter with one voice: "Man, there is death in the pot!" It's horrible! And only by quickly mixing spiced flour into the stew to thicken it up and neutralize the loathsome taste, does the resourceful host somehow manage to save the day and satisfy his hungry guests.

When things go sour

Now the point of telling this story is to remind us all that sometimes things go dreadfully wrong.

Whether we're talking about a creative culinary experiment that backfires, some late-night prank that turns unexpectedly nasty, or else a relationship that goes wrong, we need to be alert to the real possibility that, sooner or later, we will all get into sudden and unexpected difficulties.

It's the same with our spiritual explorations. Just as most of us are alert to the dangers of substance abuse, unsafe sexual practices, or even crossing a busy road without looking, so there are some spiritual experiments that are risky and some experiences that can be harmful to us. Not everything is as safe and innocuous as it may at first appear.

Beware!

For instance there are some individuals and groups who wish to profit from, or control, spiritual seekers. So beware those who wish to know all the details of your private life, or who demand to have large amounts of your money, possessions, or spare time.

As a rule of thumb, if you try something that leaves you with a bad taste in your mouth or the feeling that something isn't quite right, then just stop and think carefully before you go any further. If someone is attempting to tell you that other individuals or groups are somehow unacceptable, or of lesser worth than you are, then there is something amiss. Likewise if people try to tell you that you are less significant or valuable than other people.

Avoid bad religion

There are some theologies and religious practices that encourage negative thinking, damaging self-images, or that are psychologically harmful to your developing personal identity. If you find yourself being told that you are more "sinful" than other people, that you ask "too many questions," or that you must conform to beliefs that deny the value of all or part of humanity, or the beauty of the world around you, then it might be wise to talk to someone you trust from outside that particular group.

Just as there is some bad religion – to say nothing of bad cooking! – it's important to realize that there are religious and spiritual practices which are very affirmative and healthy for some people, but which other people might find negative and unhelpful. It's also true that there are some spiritual practices that can be unhelpful or even profoundly destructive to our inner being.

Don't feel driven or compelled

So make sure you keep your eyes and heart open, and your mind in gear. If you come away from an event or activity feeling confused, belittled, angry, hurt, or unhappy – or if you have any doubts of any kind – then speak with someone you trust.

The things of the divine spirit, or "of God," are usually always gentle: *leading* and *inviting* us on to further exploration. If you feel *driven, compelled, or forced* into a particular activity or way of thinking – then get some advice.

What is your experience?

- What spiritual activities, practices, and rituals have you tried?
- How were these positive or negative experiences for you?
- To what extent did they impact upon your spiritual development and personal identity?

Try these recipes

- As you work through the suggestions in this book keep a

record of what works and what doesn't.

- Think about those times in your life when you have felt obliged to do something or have made a decision that you really didn't want to make. Then contrast these occasions with those times when you've freely chosen, or "felt called," or "it felt natural" to do something. What were each set of feelings like? Learn to recognize or *discern* the difference between them. It'll certainly stand you in good stead in the future.

The Essentials: in a Nutshell

It's time to summarize the ground we've covered so far.

Essential 1: There's a clear connection between spirituality and personality.

- We all have different personalities and this affects the way we are as spiritual people.
- It's vital to be the person you are as honestly and authentically as you can.

Essential 2: It's important to try out different approaches.

- The only way to proceed is to experiment and discover your own needs and tastes.
- You probably like to eat three times a day, so make a similar regular commitment to exploring your spirituality.

Essential 3: Look for the free food that's out there.

- Life itself is a free gift. It's also a terminal condition that we have to learn to embrace and celebrate.
- The antidote to our mortality is to learn to say "Yes" to the opportunities for creative risk-taking that life offers us.

Essential 4: Making bread.

- The business of bread making is a good analogy for the process of engaging with the essential ingredients of your life.
- The process of nurturing your own spirituality is essentially organic. Learn to keep it fresh.

Essential 5: There's death in the pot! Sometimes.

- Be prepared for occasional disasters. And don't get

disheartened when they happen.

- Be alert to those spiritual beliefs and practices that make you feel bad about yourself or other people.
- Never be afraid to speak confidentially with someone you trust about the issues that worry you.

What is your own experience?

- Which of these five essentials strikes you as the most relevant to you at the moment?
- What does living a really authentic life it mean for you?

Try these recipes

- Write a short note to yourself outlining what you feel about your life and the sort of person you would like to be in the future. Seal it in an envelope and open it only when you have worked through this book to your satisfaction.
- Be alert to the likelihood that, by the time you reach the end of this book, you will have discerned additional or alternative "essentials" of your own. Remember that each of us is wonderfully different and that we must take responsibility for our own spiritual development.

The Recipes

Main Courses

Work: Life's Ordinary Daily Fare

There's a whole lot been written about the place of work in our daily lives. For the fortunate few, work is creative and fulfilling. But for many others – the majority of people across the globe – it is soul destroying labor and remorseless toil: a necessary evil to earn enough (and often not enough!) to live on and allow people some small time for rest and relaxation. Even in the West, most work on production lines and check-outs, in factories, in service industries, and even at desks in front of computer screens, is often routine and boring.

From our earliest schools days we are prepared for the reality of the work-a-day world. Willingly or not, we learn to invest real time, physical labor, and emotional effort into our work and, for most of us, it's the biggest commitment of our lives. It contributes hugely to our identity, dignity, and self-respect. We might complain about it endlessly, but when we don't have work, when we are unemployed, retired, or prevented from working by illness or disability, we can miss it dreadfully.

Work takes many forms but, whatever work we do, most of us do it because we have to. There's an inescapability about it. Indeed, some religious believers understand that work and toil only came into the world as the result of wrong doing, and that it's only through relentless hard work that we can ever earn our reward. (See Genesis chapter 3:23.)

Thank God it's Friday

Whatever our take on this particular story, work can certainly feel like remorseless toil! We so look forward to the evenings, the weekends, and the holidays. To those moments when our time is finally ours to enjoy in whatever ways we prefer to relax.

Infact, some religious people separate work off from what is "holy" and "sacred." Indeed the word "holiday" was originally "holy day" when work was reduced or suspended in honor of a particular saint or festival. Other people talk of work as part of the "seamless whole" of life, whereby it is simply part of the integrity of the daily cycle of our existence and cannot be separated out from it.

But whatever forms our contribution to society takes and whether we feel it is creatively fulfilling, or plain monotonous grind, our work *can* be an opportunity for our spiritual growth.

Learning to be fully present

Think about it for a moment. By being aware of how we are at work, our attentiveness to what we are doing, our need to concentrate and *be present to* the task in hand, are all essential skills that are directly relevant to our spiritual development.

Practicing the art of "being present" to our work can help us deepen our ability to live in the present moment. For it teaches us to be alert to how time, in the form of a stream of uniquely present moments, passes before us and disappears, never to be repeated. This profoundly spiritual discipline of "practicing the present moment" helps us recognize the tendency we all have to live "in the past" and "for the future," and so miss something vital about living in the present.

Learning to be in the "present moment" allows us to discover and experience a heightened sense of the mystery, wonder, and enchantment of "ordinary" daily life. This is why spiritual folk down the ages have tended to class work and prayer in the same category. For both are the two halves of the spiritual life.

Affirming human dignity

And yet equally there is also a real danger in spiritualizing monotonous or exploitative work. And the danger is that it could easily serve to encourage people to passively accept exploitative and demeaning working conditions, rather than actively critiquing the systems behind such labor, and so change things. For while everyone has a right to use their labor to contribute to the common good, no-one wants to see the human exploitation that is sadly rife in so many parts of our world.

Yet perhaps too there is a sense in which practicing the art of being fully present to our work might also cause us to think hard not only about the linkage between our own work and our contribution to society, but also about the need to stand and act in solidarity with those who are oppressed.

What is your own experience?
- What is your experience of work at this moment in time?
- What have you observed about the way parents and older friends go about the business of work?
- Are you happy with the balance in your life between work and rest?
- What are your thoughts and feelings about work as you

prepare for your working life?

Try these recipes

- Try spending two minutes in the middle of your day practicing attentiveness. No matter where you are, stop and be still. Be as alert as you can to the present moment.
- Use the "mindfulness" exercise from the Chapter on "Spiritual Snacks and Energy Drinks."
- Find out about the origins of the clothes you are wearing. Who made them? Were the workers fairly paid for their labor?

Rest

Centuries ago there was a young and very keen monk who was so determined to succeed at the serious business of becoming holy and leading a devout life that he spent every single waking moment on his knees in prayer. He ate and drank little and regularly immersed himself all night in icy sea water to ensure his "bodily appetites" were always under control. He was seriously "spiritually fit." Or so he thought.

One day he decided to visit a much-respected senior monk to seek extra wisdom and to check out his own spiritual progress. When he got to the man's house in the forest he found him lying in the sunshine with his feet on a bench and a mug of beer in his hand.

The young monk was appalled and immediately asked what the older monk thought he was doing! "Relaxing," came the reply. And when he saw the deep frown on the young monk's brow, he added: "Have you never heard it said that a well-lived spiritual life is like a well-kept longbow? If the bowstring is constantly taut then the bow becomes unfit for purpose and is useless. Likewise the soul if it never learns to rest."

Twenty-four hour culture

We live in a world that is increasingly "non-stop," with shops and other "leisure" facilities open around the clock. In many parts of the Western world research is showing that people, especially children, are getting less and less sleep as they spend more and more time watching late night TV, listening to music, and surfing the net in their bedrooms. And the result is more stress, poorer concentration, physical exhaustion, and even depression. While the analogy between the soul and a bowstring may sound very dated, the principle is still the same for us today. Rest is a crucial part of life.

Learning how to rest

A spiritual life is one which seeks to maintain a balance between the busyness of our daily routines and the need to rest and relax our mind, body, and spirit. This was never better encapsulated than in a famous slogan advertising a particular chocolate bar which, if consumed daily, the manufacturers argued, "helps you work, rest, and play." Indeed the ancient rabbis of the Jewish faith, centuries before this, taught that even God would spend eight hours each day working to maintain the universe, eight hours studying scripture, and eight hours resting and playing in the oceans with the sea monster Leviathan.

It's not for nothing that a "Sabbath day" of rest is commanded in Judaism. And in today's world, where people are increasingly in thrall to the very technology that was meant to make our lives easier and more content, the truly subversive character of the concept of a Sabbath becomes apparent. For the Hebrew word "shavat" suggests not only a period of cessation from work but, more particularly, a time when *different rules and priorities apply.*

"No time to stand and stare?"

For although the world and its ad men would seek to make us restless consumers who find our fulfillment in retail therapy alone, the requirement to spend some time (and only our time) "doing nothing" is far from being a recipe for the mind-numbing boredom that so many of us seem to dread.

William H. Davies's famous line: "A poor life this if, full of care, we have no time to stand and stare,"[4] has never rung more true for most of us today. By learning –daring ourselves– to sit quietly or stand still, and to let go of our desire to consume and possess everything and everyone, and to just be and "enjoy the moment," we can create or cultivate within us a space of rest and stress-free tranquility. A "Sabbath moment" of re-creation for our souls and bodies that allows us to touch base with reality, and to explore a different agenda, and an alternative way of being.

What is your own experience?

- Do you sleep for as long as you need to?
- How do you rest each day?
- What is your work-life balance like?
- What is your experience of boredom?

Try these recipes

- In your note book keep a record of your routine for a few days. Every fifteen or thirty minutes note how you are spending your time. Is it "work," "rest," or "play?"
- Visit a busy shopping mall and find a corner to sit or stare. What do you see?
- Begin to consider what an alternative way of being and living might be for you.
- Try this Buddhist adage: "Don't just do something. Stand there!"

Play: Party Time for the Soul

We all need to rest, relax, and chill out in whatever ways we can. And it matters little whether our preferred option is painting or cookery, sport or going out clubbing, listening to music or being still, rock climbing or scuba diving, gardening or knitting. The fact is that each of us needs to learn how to nurture those particular things that bring joy and fulfillment to our inner spirit and that teach our hearts to delight in appreciation and celebration of our existence.

The knack, the skill that we need to practice, is to learn to distinguish between those things that bring us a short-term satisfaction, "buzz," or "high," from the things that enrich us long-term and that change the way we see ourselves. It's the difference between that extra sugary or alcoholic drink, or cigarette, that may relax us and give us confidence in company, and that self-understanding that helps us to appreciate ourselves for who we really are and to rejoice in our own fundamental uniqueness and special purpose in the world.

Party time for the soul

So what is it that delights your soul? What is it that brings you pleasure and makes you feel really alive?

Chances are that, whatever your answer to these questions, the feelings of delight and pleasure you experience are the direct result of the harmonizing – the integration – of your bodily-physical self with your mental-spiritual self. This is so important! For those people who would seek to separate their embodied self from their mental and spiritual self – like the young monk in the previous story – are failing to understand what it really means to be human.

Foot loose and fancy free?

Of course, most of the world's religions, fearing the outcomes of uninhibited pleasure and delight, have always urged restraint. Indeed those religions which allegedly encouraged "orgiastic abandon" (the secret rites supposedly used by the followers of Bacchus, for instance) have always had a bad press.

There is an intimate connection between the fear of (people) being out of control and the idea of divine *dis*-pleasure and *dis*-satisfaction. At least as far as any "traditional," "orthodox," and "patriarchal" God is portrayed. For pleasure and delight have generally been directly associated with "misuse," with "waste," and, therefore by extension, with immorality.

The very idea of "waste" – from the Latin "vastus" – suggests those dangerous, desolate, wild, boundary-less places, "wastes" and "waste-lands," that are *outside the control* of all civilizing influences, order and authority. So the idea that "decent" and "proper" religion and spirituality might encourage people to relinquish their self-control and will power has been routinely seen as *waste*ful and, therefore, deplorable.

"Wasting time with God"

And yet there is something very restorative and "soul making" about exploring the tension between re-creation and recreation. For playing – doing things without any particular purpose or end – opens up a space inside us for imagining new possibilities for ourselves, and for seeing the world differently. And, as such, play is something far too important to be left behind in adolescence. We need to rediscover a "play-full" attitude to life.

Perhaps each of us should be exploring outside our own self-imposed boundaries and finding urgent and re-creative ways to "waste more time with God" and so allow the spirit of the divine to *play* on our hearts and minds, and invite us to join more passionately in the irrepressible game of life.

Learning to laugh

The New Testament recounts that "Jesus wept" (John 11:35) but not that he laughed. Indeed, unless it's laughing at other people to mock and belittle them, laughter isn't big in the world's religions. Yet surely Jesus and the other prophets and gurus laughed? After all, laughing makes people feel so much better! And perhaps it's our need today to learn to laugh as never before, that is the reason why stand-up comedy is getting very big on TV everywhere. Perhaps there's a lesson for us here.

For there's something very "cathartic" and very liberating and refreshing about the ability of a stand-up comedian to take ideas and incidents from everyday life and get her audience to see things in a different light. And about the genius of improvisation that enables the comic to interact with a live audience and bring an unscripted authenticity that is genuinely able to engage us "body and soul." By presenting us with typical human dilemmas and highlighting the absurdity of certain kinds of behaviors and responses, she deflates our self-important egos and gently chides us into seeing things differently. Our laughter at our own behavior is both the "penance" imposed on us and the "sacramental" means, by which we are opened up to new and healing forms of self awareness.

The parallels between stand-up comedy and the parables of Jewish and Christian scripture, as well as with good ritual or worship, are there for all to see. For the "point" of all three is to enable or to *trigger* a change in perception that enlarges our vision and self-understanding and helps us move on.

Finding "soul time"

For we move on and are changed by growing with each new experience. And just as children learn and acquire experience by playing, so all of us can learn so much about ourselves by spending time on activities that release us from our regular daily constraints and bring us to a place of strange newness and delightful – playful – novelty. Here it is that our soul, our inner self, finds the ingredients it needs to be broken apart, re-created, nurtured, and enlarged. Here we may learn to dance and play to a different tune, and find ourselves surprise guests at a party that might change our life forever.

What is your own experience?

- What gives you a real buzz and a high? Be honest with yourself.
- What is it that brings you pleasure, delights your soul, and makes you feel really alive?
- Is there a difference between your answers to these two questions? Why is that?
- When was the last time you had a really good laugh? Try to recall the occasion.
- When was the last time you felt that your horizons or your self-awareness were suddenly enlarged? What did you learn from this experience? How might it be repeated?

Try these recipes

- If you don't yet have a hobby or pastime then look at what's available locally. Really dare yourself to try something completely different. Or something you've always wanted to do. See what happens.

- Set aside some time to "waste with God" or on some activity that may appear to be pointless, but which takes you outside your usual routines. See what happens.
- What would be the ingredients for your "party of a lifetime"? Who would be on the guest list?
- Now imagine you get an unexpected invitation to a party organized in order to change the world. What contribution could you make to the arrangements? Spend some time day-dreaming what this party would be like.
- Are there steps you could take now to make this sort of difference to the world around you?

Art, Music, and the Creative Stuff

Most of us will have had the experience of compulsory art, craft, or music lessons during our school days. And for many of us they will have proved a mixed blessing. Somehow the necessity of being creative "on demand" for an hour's class first thing after lunch is almost guaranteed to backfire! Consequently it comes as little surprise that many of us struggle to express ourselves creatively. "I'm not artistic!" is sadly not an untypical response from far too many of us. Yet it remains profoundly true that there is a creative streak in all of us somewhere, if we can release it.

Lighting the spark

For the native Aboriginal people of Australia the return to their traditional homelands after decades of exile was the trigger for an enormous burgeoning of creative expression. It was as though the reconnection with their ancestral lands released the flow of a long-dormant spiritual energy which was then expressed through stunning painting and beautiful craftwork. Being once again in touch with what sustained them spiritually allowed their creativity to flourish.

The performance of a life-time

Most days I am treated to a display of improvised dance by our small daughter. While she is verbally highly articulate, is making good progress with her reading and writing, and her paintings are nothing if not "colorful," it's when she decides to dance that something extraordinary happens. For, even though she has had no dance tuition, when the music of her favorite tracks and movies is played she can't resist getting to her feet. Her body engages with the music with astonishingly nuanced and synchro-nized moves, gestures, and rhythms that form her creative response to what she is experiencing. And while she sometimes allows us to watch, it's clear that her performance is largely meant to be a private exploration of her developing sense of identity, embodiment, and the desire to express the creative urges within her.

It's exactly the same for those many people who enjoy going out clubbing with friends. For the music and the ambiance have the power to prompt improvised dancing which, impermanent and "one-off" or "disposable" as it is, is also a highly creative art form.

Indeed dance and the other "performance" arts, like music, alert us to the fact that life itself can be rightly said to be a creative art form that we perform with myriad random acts of daily living. With each new day we can choose how to approach the performance of our routines: whether or not to include particular gestures of compassion or tenderness with friends and family, flourishes of openness or closure with strangers, and new ideas, or acts of solidarity or concern, for the great issues and dilemmas that affect everyone on the planet.

While William Shakespeare wrote that "all the world's a stage,"[5] the performance of *our own* life-time is a uniquely personal and richly spiritual task that deserves our loving attention and commitment.

Creativity and Spirituality
Whatever form our creativity takes – painting, music, gardening, cookery, origami, or dancing – it's pretty obvious that creativity and spirituality go hand in hand: whether or not we happen to be religious. The two phenomena nurture each other naturally. If we are creative people we will recognize how the expression of our gift makes our spirit sing within us, and that we have a profound, visceral, need to do what we do.

Good spirituality also demands the nurture and expression of that creative dimension of our inner self. It's partly about our being embodied creatures who experience the world through our senses and express our response in random acts of creativity. But it's also about the nature of creativity itself.

"The dangerous edge of things"
For in expressing ourselves creatively, in sitting down to produce a piece of art, transforming a corner of earth into a flowerbed or vegetable patch, or knitting a scarf for a friend, we are creating something new and original. We don't have to be artistic geniuses, but by being creative we are opening ourselves up to the spirit within us or beyond us. We are engaging with "otherness." And that "otherness" may be variously defined as "God," or "divinity," or simply as the "creative spirit within." Indeed, an individual's encounter with her creativity may also be described as an experience of the "What-she-is-not-yet," or "What-she-wishes," or even "What-she-fears-and-dreads-to-explore."

It's in this sense that our creativity puts us on what the

English poet Robert Browning calls the "dangerous edge of things,"[6] because creativity (like prayer, as we'll discover later) is about moving from what is known to what is unknown. Being creative is about expressing whatever we find within ourselves. And that can be dark and risky as much as it might be bright and wonderful.

Shining in the darkness

Creativity, like spirituality, is about making ourselves open to possibility and novelty: to what doesn't yet exist. Whether it be the object we have not yet created or the person we are yet to become. For it is by following the creative urge, intuition, or feeling we sense inside us that we become more fully who we are, or are meant to be. Being creative is about letting, or daring, ourselves be drawn into a liminal place where anything may happen. A mysterious "dark" place at the frontier or boundary of our human selfhood, knowledge, or experience. A generative space for birthing those new things that will never cease coming into our lives if we let them and that allow us to imagine ourselves anew in ways we could had never foreseen or to which we had never dared aspire.

What is your own experience?
- Make a list of the ways that you feel you are creative.
- What sorts of response do music, dance, song, or art create in you?
- What does it feel like when you express your creativity?
- What things do you aspire to be and do?

Try these recipes
- If you don't yet do anything creative then dare yourself to

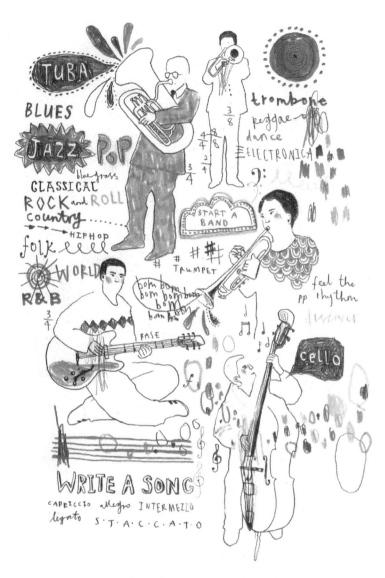

try something for a few hours each week.

- Play some music that speaks to you powerfully, and in the privacy of your room, trying moving your body to the rhythms of what you hear. Be aware of what happens.
- Find a piece of art, music, or a landscape that "grabs" your soul and moves you deeply. Build time into your weekly

schedule to be with some of these things. Experience their power within you and try to respond in some way.

- Try to explore the "liminal space" between "where you are" and "where you are not yet." It may be a physical or mental space for solitude, a real place that puts you on the edge of your comfort zone, or a commitment to a regular time of creativity, silent prayer, or meditation. What does this feel like? How might you explore this further?

Relationships – Made in Heaven?

Anyone who works with children and young people will be alert to how central relationships are to human development. Very young children find no inconsistency in having several "best friends" in one day, while older children experience the intense desire to be part of "the in-crowd" and the pressure on those who refuse to conform. In later teenage years particular special friendships test out our capacity to relate in more mature ways and these may, in turn, lead to longer term or even life-long commitments. What is clear in all of this is that a pretty essential part of what it means to be human is bound up with the need for relationships.

We all need to be needed

Right from our earliest time in our mother's womb we need to connect with others. This is both a basic survival strategy and the chief means whereby we discover who we are as individuals. And if we're honest with ourselves, we all know that some of our motivation to be and act as we do is all about our deep desire to be needed: to give and to receive positive emotional responses. Indeed it is through our relationships with other people that we find our fulfillment and flourishing. So it's really not surprising that so much of our lives revolves around creating and recreating relationships and connections.

Hard-wired for friendship

While sooner or later we may choose to devote ourselves to a committed relationship with a particular individual, we will normally expend a considerable amount of energy developing friendships with a whole range of very different people. And anyone who has taken time to consider why some friendships work and others don't will have realized that there is more to such relationships that common interests or shared personality traits.

The key to good friendships is the recognition that friendship requires not only a commitment to mutuality, respect, and frequent compromise, but to working at the dynamic of the relationship itself. Friendships need to be continually renewed and never taken for granted. And while that's often really hard work, ultimately it's worth it. Just think how infinitely less our lives would be if we hadn't a friend in the world!

Making friends of our parents and lovers

This need to work at creating life-giving friendships applies just as much to our parents and long-term partners. If the hardest transition we have to navigate in life is the business of making friends of our parents once we've grown up and moved out, not far behind must surely come the daunting task of remaining friends with the person we have committed ourselves to after years of daily familiarity.

For while we are very good at celebrating the thrill of falling in love and the excitement of setting out on a new and fresh relationship with someone we love, there is a fragility about long-term relationships that also needs recognition. Relationships can so easily become stale, lifeless, and even hurtful. And this happens when we fail to work at the dynamics of the relationship, when we begin to take the other for granted; when we cease to be friends.

Better to be loved or liked?

All this points to an often overlooked aspect of human relationships: the difference between liking and loving. We tend to assume that it's better to love than to like – and perhaps it is. But in too readily promoting the need to *love* our friends, neighbors, and, even, our enemies, we can too easily pass over the implications of our capacity *simply to like someone*. This is true whether or not we happen to be religious people.

For, while the knowledge that we are loved is fundamentally supportive and liberating, the idea that we are *actually liked* is tremendously creative and empowering in a different sort of way. Of course it may be that we both like and love a particular individual, but discerning and acknowledging the difference is still important.

Think of someone you might love out of a sense of duty (Aunt Mildred, Uncle George, the elderly couple next door) and then of someone *you actually like*, just because you really like them. Think about it for a moment. Then turn the thought around. Imagine that someone loves you because they must and, next, that someone likes you simply because they do. Can you *feel* the difference?

Of course the need to be liked and popular, the buzz of having friends and admirers, can become a drug for our ego and have a very negative effect on our spiritual development. It could make us very selfish and out-of-touch with reality. So we need to be gently alert to the operation of this tendency. But just for now let's take those positive feelings and work with them a little more.

It's spiritual, stupid!

Just imagine that, if there were a God or Great Creator Spirit, this God didn't just love you because that's what the script says should happen. Imagine, instead, that this God *actually likes you* and wants to get to know you better. Or else, if you don't believe in God, imagine that Creation itself is friendly; because you are literally a part of each other. That when you stare into the amazing vastness of the universe you are touched by a sense of oneness and connection that resonates deeply and stirs up something within you. That the magical enchantment you experience under a starry night sky grabs your attention as viscerally and powerfully as any exciting human relationship and makes your soul sing. How does that feel?

Our capacity to love and to like, our ability to connect and relate to others, our facility and desire for friendship, are spiritual gifts of great importance. *But they are given not for our sake alone.* The spiritual task that daily faces each of us is to discern how to live out these gifts not only in our own lives and relationships, but in the local communities and global networks of which we are a part.

And the ultimate challenge comes when we ask ourselves, what are the limits of our desire to relate and create friendships? The ultimate goal is surely to do all we can to stretch our relating to include those who are most in need of our love and our liking. Who are those people for us? Where does our friendship and concern stop?

On active listening

Whatever the nature of the relationships we have, one of the greatest differences we can make is when we decide to *really listen* to what people are saying to us. One of the commonest complaints made by those who feel ignored, over-looked, or excluded – be they lovers, friends, neighbors, or people living on the margins of society – is that "nobody listens." If you doubt this then try spending sometime in the company of someone who needs to talk. Be present to them and be really attentive to what they're saying. Show with your body language that what they have to say *actually matters* to you. And watch the impact good listening has.

Our ability to listen well and "actively" can make a huge

difference, not only to our own relationships, but to the promotion of peaceful relations all over our world and to the overcoming of those pernicious mechanisms of exclusion and control that daily undermine the future of humanity. We urgently need to practice the art of active listening in a world where everyone appears to be shouting at each other.

What is your own experience?

- What do you think your friends value about you?
- What are your memories of being loved and liked?
- Can you recall a time when someone really listened to you? How did it feel?
- What is your experience of the more "universal" dimension of friendship?
- What are the limits of your friendship? How far can you comfortably stretch it?
- What might happen if you were to go beyond this comfort zone?

Try these recipes

- Take some time to consider what's "good" about the best relationships you have.
- Have a coffee with a fellow student whom you don't know. See what happens.
- Go and spend some time volunteering with a local agency and meet some new people who have nothing to do with your life on campus. Allow yourself to listen hard to what they're saying.

Naughty or Nice? The Delights of Embodied Experience

The back story

Food and sex have always been intimately connected both with the language of the divine and with human culture. The urge to consume in order to survive and the urge to reproduce represent two fundamental aspects of what it means to be human. Despite the fact that, for a fortunate few of us in the so-called "developed world," we don't need to struggle to find food, and sex is now no longer necessary simply to ensure the continuation of our species, food and sex remain very strong forces within our psyches. Particularly the sex drive, which is so powerful that all sorts of social taboos have been created and enshrined in our religious and culture values and practices, with the sole purpose of controlling it. Thus human sexuality has generally either been "sanctified" or "demonized." If we wish to be holy, then we must deny or sublimate our sexual drives. For to "give in" to the temptations of sexual activity risks forever cutting us off from the "more important" *religious* purposes and goals of this "earthly" life.

And within some religious groups, this tendency is still active even today, and focused around the debate regarding what is "natural" and "normal." Some religious commentators will go to enormous lengths to interpret scriptural texts to illustrate "divine" approval or disapproval of particular types of sexual identity and practice.

There is no doubt though that good spirituality (and good religion for that matter) takes very seriously, and positively, the delights of embodied experience. But what does this mean exactly?

We are creatures with bodies. We are creatures *who are bodies*: with senses – and, moreover, with imagination! Creatures who are made for relationships and who need the warmth and love of other human beings. Wherever we are on the spectrum of gender and sexuality, the urge to explore and express – or else deny and repress – our body's desires will be something that cannot fail to grab our attention, day or night!

"Erotic": good, or bad, or what?

"Erotic" is a word that has, sadly, been almost entirely lost to pornographers. In essence "erotic" simply means that positive, primal, or visceral energy that exists between people: a child at its mother's breast, a couple in a deep and long-established relationship who often intuit each other's feelings, and between complete strangers who are attracted to each other - for whatever reason. It has also been argued that this same energy flows between a healer and the person who is healed.

The first important thing to remember is that the erotic energy within our own being that flows, often unbidden, between us and other people - is a normal and natural part of who we are as human beings. The second thing is that it's up to us to decide whether, when, and how to express this energy in terms of sexual desire or activity, artistic endeavor, or social justice. There is no inevitability that the erotic must lead to the sexual. Sexual activity will always remain a non compulsory option! *And we should never feel obliged to do something we don't want to do.*

However, when it comes to sexual expression, people generally find themselves making decisions at a non-rational or gut level. What's essential then is that they take good care not to do anything they might regret later. And, as a rule of thumb, when things get physical, it's generally not the best idea to rely too much on the protection of wishful thinking, prayers, or patron saints! Better to get some more trustworthy form of protection for our sexual and emotional health. (See the chapter "First Aid, Help, and Hygiene.")

Body and soul – flesh and spirit
People have argued for centuries about the relationship between

body and soul, and flesh and spirit. And while there is a fascinating debate about whether we even have a soul – and where it's located – and how it might be different from our heart or mind, it's clear that we are more than just flesh. Our critical self-consciousness and our ability to imagine alternative ways of being and living suggest that, in some curious way, we appear to be something more.

Yet it's our bodies and senses that give us the means of experiencing the world. And our bodies are also part of our self-identity. We have bodies – indeed *we are bodies* – and they manifest our inner self-consciousness, and are central to our personal identity and capacity to act in the world.

So when we adorn our body: with make-up, tattoos, body art, piercings, and all the latest fashions, accessories, and hairstyles, we are making a statement about how we see and appreciate ourselves as unique individuals in the world. The ways in which we "inscribe" or embellish our skin and treat and value our physical bodies, is an intrinsic dimension of our spirituality. Though it's also vital to remember that we must be alert to the real tendency for false images of physical beauty, body shape, and appearance to be projected and promoted within society at large. Loveliness, attractiveness, and beauty are ultimately much more than the way we look. Every individual is a person of unique splendor, regardless of their bodily appearance and ability.

Gender and sexuality
We must also learn to value our gender and sexuality as part of our physical and spiritual make-up.

While there may often be periods when we struggle to accept both or either, and need time to explore what they mean for us, wholeness comes through accepting and being comfortable with our gendered nature and sexual identity. And we must never allow anyone to tell us otherwise.

Integrating physicality, sexuality, and spirituality

What's important for the spiritual journey is that we each decide how to *integrate* our embodied experience, sexuality, and spirituality so that they become honest, authentic, and complementary aspects of our being "at ease" with ourselves and each other, and enriching who we are as people.

This doesn't automatically mean accepting that "anything goes," sexually or spiritually speaking, and eliminating all our boundaries, concerns, and uncertainties. Integrating our physical and sexual selves with our spirituality does mean, however, that, in our own good time, we can come to being open to, and happy about, the fact that erotic energy, sexual feelings, and physical pleasure are nothing to be ashamed of and, indeed, are there to be explored and enjoyed in a way and at a time that feels right for each of us.

Decoding the jargon

In the realm of sexuality and spirituality, just like in the world of cookery, there is a certain amount of jargon and technical terminology that needs decoding. For, often, terms are used that are misunderstood or whose meanings have changed considerably over time.

Let's take some time to examine some often misunderstood terms.

Celibacy/celibate:	For those who may have had a sexual relationship in the past, but who have promised or vowed not to express their erotic energy in a sexual way. So they commit to remaining single or unattached.
Chastity/chaste:	Some people have never, or not yet, had sex; they want it that way. It's not that uncommon. It's also clear that chastity describes the practice of faithful monogamy within a committed relationship.
Desire:	Those feelings, wishes, and longings all people experience to identify with, have, or possess someone, something, or some

state. Some people and religions see desire as the root of all human dilemmas and, consequently, something to be eliminated.

Embodiment: The natural state of human beings. We experience the world through our bodies, senses, and feelings. To suppress all of these feelings is unlikely to result in wholeness and flourishing.

Erotic: That positive, primal, or visceral energy flowing between individuals. It may also be experienced when we engage with wonderful art and music, read great literature, dance, or enjoy good food, or the wonders of the natural world.

Fantasy: Most people have fantasies – sexual or otherwise – though few admit it. It's perfectly normal but, if you're worried about yours, then speak with a trusted friend.

Gender: Biologically there are men and women: and quite a few people (more than you'd imagine!) who that feel that these terms don't describe who they really are. It's high time we learned to value and celebrate the embodied experience of all people, regardless of their biology.

Guilt: Those feelings of self-criticism for mistakes, faults, and oversights that need acknowledgment and apology. Failure to deal with guilt can lead to feelings of *shame* which can easily become internalized, seriously destructive, and prevent human flourishing. Saying sorry

	– to yourself and others – and then moving on, is always best. Talk to someone if you need to.
Honesty:	Transparency of expectations and openness to truth. All healthy relationships have honesty, sincerity, and integrity at their heart. Being honest with ourselves is the beginning of spiritual wisdom.
Love:	A feeling of fondness and concern that people have and share. Love may be non-sexual: for a parent, friend, or child, or expressed sexually and passionately for an individual, or take the form of concern for justice and equality for needy individuals or groups across the world. Loving ourselves – *self-love* – is that necessary degree of respect and liking for ourselves which is a sign of mature self-understanding.
Lust:	The eagerness to posses or desire something or someone, usually sexually. The majority of people experience lustful thoughts. And it's a powerful force that can easily take us to places and actions we may later regret. So the golden rule is always "do no harm to yourself or to others!"
Masturbation:	It used to be regarded as a form of moral depravity and sexual self-abuse, but nowadays is often seen as the ultimate in safe sex. It may also be regarded as a natural way of exploring human embodiment and of connecting sexuality and

	spirituality.
Monogamy:	Sticking with one partner. Committed long term relationships are generally agreed to be most fulfilling, but I know some loving people who admit they just can't manage it. That's not to say that committed relationships the second or third time round don't produce really good, creative, and blessed relationships.
"Open" relationships:	Uncomfortable though it may be for those of us whose experience is only with "traditional" or monogamous relationships, be they "straight" or "same sex," there are people whose commitment to each other finds no problem with sexual activity outside that relationship.
"Sex before":	While it may seem sensible to explore our bodies and experiment with our sexuality before choosing a committed relationship, I've met people who have had so many short-term liaisons that they can't find fulfillment with one individual. Each of us is different, yet it is so very easy – and commonplace – to be judgmental about what ultimately is a very personal and private matter.
Sexuality:	"Gay," "Lesbian," "Bi-sexual," and "Straight," describe people's sexuality. Far too many people judge others according to these labels. Religious folk particularly should stop using their scriptures as a tool of condemnation. Let's learn to accept people as people.
Responsibility:	Taking responsibility for our own actions

is the central most important element to a mature and integrated spirituality. Those of us concerned with good religion and spirituality might consider what our responsibility is to promote healing, integration, and justice for everyone!

What is your own experience?

- What do you feel about the body that is you?
- How have you experienced the tension between "body" and "spirit?"
- What part does your embodied self play in shaping your own spirituality?
- What would you like to say to yourself on the subject of your sexuality?

Try these recipes

- Find two or three new stimuli that you enjoy for each of your five senses – touch, sight, taste, sound, and smell. Make a list of these and share them with a trusted friend.
- Spend a few minutes each day using each of your senses in turn to experience and enjoy the world around you. Make a note of anything that strikes you.

Travel

These days with gap years as well as long summer vacations students and young people venture further than ever and, with cheap travel, just about anywhere is very much open and accessible to anyone. As never before the world is our backyard to enjoy as and when we choose and taking time out to travel the world has become a common rite of passage for many, often to the consternation of parents who have forgotten their own youthful adventures.

Have plastic, will travel

Even though foreign travel has never been easier, with a knowledge of English and a major credit card opening so many doors across the globe, there's still a sense in which real travel broadens the mind and offers experiences that mere armchair or virtual travel in cyberspace cannot hope to rival.

For there's something wonderfully exhilarating about exploration and encountering things for the first time with our own eyes, ears, noses, and taste buds. To say nothing of what travel can do for our sense of our own identity and place in the world.

Boldly going

Any history book, travelogue, or sci-fi film will tell us that a fascination with journeying and adventure has always been central to human identity. For journeying into strangeness, newness, and difference offers a pretty elemental experience, a thrill that grabs us viscerally: fear and curiosity mixed in equal measure with a buzz that can only be appreciated by those who've already "been there, done that, and got the T-shirt!" These kinds of encounters remain one of the greatest experiences available to us, even though we should never expect things to be all "plain sailing."

The word "travel" has its origins in the word "travail." It suggests that something akin to the elemental pain and labor of childbirth awaits those who want the real thing. Not only physical hardships and discomfort, but the spiritual exhilaration of meeting staggering beauty and raw, untested experience and new life.

Encountering difference

The very facts of crossing boundaries and frontiers, and speaking in a foreign language, require us to risk what is familiar and safe. Travel is about discovering the routes and pathways that allow us to cross back and forth over the boundary between what is safe and secure and what is perilous and risk-filled; between what-is and what-is-yet-to-be. Being a boundary walker and a voyager across frontiers requires an openness to otherness and to difference, an ability to learn to understand and express ourselves in unfamiliar languages and cultures, and a capacity to cope with what is strange and novel and which frequently reduces us to confusion and silence. If you doubt this, then take a moment to imagine yourself alone in a busy market in a country where everyone is staring at you and nobody understands your own language!

Journeys of the soul

If you can imagine doing this, you must realize that a similar openness to risk and to the unknown is demanded by those who would be spiritual wayfarers and soul travelers. For it is very often the case that the distance from our head to our heart is much greater than even the vast journeys across our continents and oceans. And frequently such journeys can take a life time. But fortunately for us, that's exactly the length of time we have available!

Rediscovering familiar places

Of course, not all travel is to places that are actually new to us. Many times in our own life we will have revisited places where we first went with our parents, or on a youthful solo expedition, only to discover that they are completely different than we remember them. The reason for this is that we are seeing them with different eyes and broader experience. And since the journey of life isn't a simple linear progression, but is rather like a spiral or helix which loops back on itself, so when we arrive at a familiar place it may often well be that we are seeing it afresh, as if for the first time, because we are seeing it from a different vantage point.

The ability to rediscover familiar places and re-evaluate what we have hitherto understood as "normal" and "ordinary" alongside what is "new" and "unusual" is an important skill that we need to cultivate. For there are many stories about people setting off on great journeys only to discover that their destination, their heart's desire, or their treasure was all the time waiting for them at home.

Take some basic equipment

Whether we are exploring what's right under our nose or journeying far from home, soul traveling is different from physical travel. It's no less real, of course, but some of the essential equipment will be different. Visiting a new country requires maps and detailed guide books. But soul travelers will usually only have their hearts as a compass and perhaps also a chart, like early sailors and pirates, to give their *relative* but not exact position.

Such charts are unique to each soul traveler. They begin from the moment of our birth and plot our course through all the highs and lows, detours and derailments, and the times of great joy and celebration that we have experienced. Moreover they form the starting point of our future journeys by helping us to stay in touch with our past travels and present stopping places.

Traveling light

But while they may give us possible clues as to our direction and destination, they can never guarantee anything, least of all a safe arrival at our destination. Nor do they insulate us from mishaps and setbacks. And whereas both globe-trotters and spiritual wayfarers will certainly have problems and dilemmas to overcome, the common quandary for soul travelers as they encounter "otherness," is to find themselves "all at sea on an ocean of possibilities," where multiple options for the future need to be discerned, plotted, and trusted.

Finding a guide

The secret with all travel is to "journey light," with as little baggage as possible to hinder us. And while some people like to travel alone, and some in the company of others, a personal guide may be of particular help for many of us.

Such a guide may be someone who uses their own experience to help us plan in advance the journey we are to make alone, someone we keep in touch with from time to time as we journey, or someone we encounter on the way, who has important "local knowledge" to share with us for a time. (See "Coffee and Cake and a Quiet Chat.")

There are always lots of things to think about before we set off. Not least the risks that lie ahead! And it never gets any easier, no matter how many times we do it. For the spiritual journey through life is always, and forever, about setting off again into the unknown. Never sure of arriving where we might wish, but confident, nonetheless, that the journey itself will be the making of us.

What is your own experience?

- Where have you traveled thus far in your life?
- What adventures and misfortunes have befallen you?
- What have your travels taught you about yourself and life in general?
- What essential pieces of equipment do you recommend for traveling?
- How may these be used to help you on your spiritual journey?

Try these recipes

- Spend some time imagining yourself alone in a real but strange country, where everyone is staring at you and nobody understands your own language. What thoughts and emotions surface for you?
- Make a chart of your spiritual journey so far. It may take any form you like: a simple list, straight, or wavy lines like a map, branches on a tree, islands in an ocean, planets in the night sky, or photos in a scrapbook.

  Begin as far back in your life as you remember. Use each line, symbol, or photo to plot the twists and turns of your journey. Note down the places where you have lived and the key, life-changing people or encounters you have known or had. List any spiritual, mental, or physical experiences you have had, as well as the "big questions" that grab your attention.

  While you may prefer to plot your journey sequentially, as a time line, don't worry if some things don't fit. Let them float or drift about. Remember to leave space for your future adventures. And be as honest as you can. This is a secret treasure chart that you will only show to those you trust!

• Do you have a hoped-for goal or desired destination for your spiritual journeying? How will you know whether you have arrived?

• What sort of guide might suit you? How will you recognize one, should one come your way?

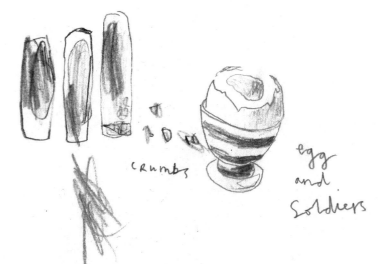

crumbs

egg
and
soldiers

Try Out these Other Recipes

Breakfasts

At the start of the day

There's nothing quite like birdsong in the stillness before dawn. Even in the city there's generally at least one bird to be heard greeting the new day. It's a magical time, especially in the spring or summer. So it's no surprise that many of the world's religions encourage prayer and meditation at daybreak when, for a short time before the busyness of the day, everything seems to pause and hold its breath in attentive expectation.

But contrast that if you will with the experience of being rudely awakened by the alarm clock and dragged from sleep in a warm bed on a cold and miserable Monday morning. That's probably the reality for so many of us! Yet how we begin the day is really important.

"Going to work on an egg"

During the 1960's the UK's Egg Marketing Board launched a TV campaign to get more people eating eggs for breakfast. Their slogan was "go to work on an egg." You can probably imagine the commercials! Yet, at the risk of sounding like one of those ads, nutritionally speaking, breakfast is probably the most significant meal of the day, especially if we eat the sorts of food that provide "slow release energy."

Put on the coffee pot

Yet while some people can't do without breakfast, others simply can't face it. For these people a shot of caffeine or a zesty fruit tea are probably the order of the day. Either way, getting something into our stomachs first thing sets us up to face the rigors of our daily schedule and goes a long way to ensuring we can concentrate, not get tetchy about our work or colleagues, and be as positive as possible.

The right sort of breakfast?

And while we should seriously consider the sorts of things that we consume physically, preferring those proteins (nuts, eggs, cheese and meat products – the least processed the better) and complex carbohydrates (leafy green vegetables and fruit) that will slowly release bursts of energy over several hours, so we should avoid beginning the day by filling our mind and soul with a diet of unhealthy self doubt, fretting about our ability to perform the tasks of the day ahead, or else by stuffing our imaginations with unwholesome fears about all the "dreadful things" that might go wrong. For the right sort of nourishment is vital for our spiritual self too.

Letting it simmer a while

Just as important as taking healthy nutrition at the start of the day is making the effort to sit awhile quietly and let ourselves "come to," shake off our drowsiness, and focus our minds and hearts on the tasks of the day ahead. For while our physical requirement for energy will be met by the nourishment we consume, our spiritual needs can be similarly addressed by creating a space in which we can "earth" ourselves and open ourselves up to the creative possibilities and challenges that the new day will hold. Whether or not we might prefer to call this "prayer," "meditation," or "mindfulness," it's an opportunity for us to "touch base" with the reality of a new day and to say "Yes" to all that life will offer us.

Saying "Yes" to life

This does not, however, mean we should adopt a fatalistic attitude to life. Nor does it mean that we have to like, or agree with, or meekly accept everything that will come our way.

Saying "Yes" to life is about *engaging positively* with each event, person, or idea that we encounter. Saying "Yes" to life is about trying to *actively embrace* newness and difference and being willing to step outside our comfort zone and see things from different perspectives. Saying "Yes" to life is about *opening ourselves* to the possibilities for things being other than they are, and then finding ourselves growing in all sorts of ways as we dare ourselves to respond.

Spiritual sustenance

Putting effort into our spiritual self care is every bit as important as looking after the physical needs we have at the start of the day. For if we take time to ground ourselves in the realization that spiritual energy is released as we open ourselves to newness, and that our spiritual selves grow as we connect to the world around us, then the day ahead of us will shine with creative possibility.

What is your own experience?

- What does your morning routine look like? Are there ways you might change it?
- What physical and spiritual sustenance do you take at the

start of the day?

- How do you approach your daily tasks and routines?

Try these recipes

- Create your own breakfast cereal using a mixture of nuts and seeds, berries or fruit, and yogurt or honey. Try a green or fruit tea – or a decaffeinated drink. Stay with these things for a week and see what happens.
- Trying getting up at daybreak and being silent in the first light of the day. Listen to the world around you as it awakes. See what it feels like.
- Endeavor to approach the new day with an air of expectation or excitement. Be open each day to discovering new things about yourself and the world.

Suppers and Midnight Snacks

Last thing at night

Recent research suggests that our late night habits of viewing TV and surfing the net are seriously affecting on our sleep patterns by reducing the amount of time we actually experience deep "REM" sleep and, so, leading to physical and mental tiredness. It seems we are determined to extend the day time and its activities to a level that is actually detrimental to our bodies and well-being. And that's ultimately unsustainable.

While this is not to suggest that it's not great fun to experience and enjoy the nightlife on offer, it's quite amazing the difference that a pattern of regular and sufficient sleep makes to our physical and spiritual health; to say nothing of the impact on our levels of efficiency.

A light supper and a soul-full night

Although it's rightly well-known that a fruit tea or milky a drink before bed are said to aid relaxation and sleep, people are generally unaware of the spiritual equivalent.

Try using the time it takes you to finish your drink to think over the events of the past day. First make a point of noting one thing that might perhaps have been done *differently*. What's important here is *not* to be judgmental with yourself. Don't criticize or blame yourself. Simply note what happened and then move on. And make sure to take time for remembering the best thing or things that happened. Allow yourself to smile a little at the memories that surface. Finally let go of the whole day by saying "thank you" to yourself – and for the life that you have enjoyed this day!

Midnight snacks

There is also research that suggests that it's really not that odd or unusual for people *not to sleep* the whole night through. That perhaps a more natural sleep pattern, one less ruled by the demands of our pressurized and clock-driven Western life-styles, is one with a break roughly half-way through the night.

Whatever the truth of the matter, many of us will be aware that we sometimes, or perhaps quite often, find ourselves awake in the middle of the night unable to sleep. Once again, while a herbal tea or cool milk or glass of water may settle our stomachs, some gentle spiritual activity may be required for our soul's ease. So here's a "mindfulness" exercise that may help.

This is an exercise that's clearly best done in bed, as it's likely to send you off to sleep! Begin by being aware of your body: its position on the flat of the bed; its length and breadth. Then, starting with your toes and working up your body, become aware of your limbs and muscles. Flex each in turn, but make sure to keep your arms in their regular comfortable sleeping position.

When you arrive at your face, take time to move each muscle, if you can. Pay special attention to the jaw and mouth and the eyes, eyebrows, and muscles in your forehead. Gently move them to and fro to make sure your eyes are gently relaxed and not screwed up. Then become aware of your breathing. Don't change it, but simply notice how it enters cold into your nostrils, and leaves them warm. Focus your whole attention on this. Let your mind's eye rest on the tip of your nose and on your breathing.

Additionally you may like to visualize a point of light. This may be imagined to be "above" you or else "below," or "deep inside" you. It doesn't matter. Concentrate on this light, but don't "analyze" or think about it rationally. In your mind's eye, simply let this light fill your whole being with its heat, warmth, and radiance. Stay with it for as long as you can and let it work its magic.

Night time blues?

Of course it may be that we are unable to sleep because of our dreams. Dreams, whether "good dreams" or "nightmares," often have a habit of breaking out of our heads and waking us up. Now while it's accepted that everyone dreams, since dreams are the way in which our brains process material – the events of the past day, our subconscious desires and needs, and our feelings – not all people are actually aware of dreaming.

Dreams may perhaps be best likened to a mental collage, or even a sort of film-clip, of actual events and experiences, repressed feelings, and unarticulated thoughts that is created as our unconscious brain sifts and categorizes our lived experience of the world. Experience suggests that if we make an effort to recall our dreams, it can be very creative and rewarding. So each time you remember a dream, try to make an actual note of it, then and there, for later consideration.

And it's important to realize that we don't need to be a Freud or a Jung to be able to make some meaningful sense of it for ourselves. For oftentimes, out of the apparent randomness of a dream, we can discover some new perspective, some new "take" on an issue or an event that concerns us. Somehow our unconscious self manages to come up with a solution, a memory, or a name that had been evading our conscious rational mind. This may well be why many religions have understood God to speak through dreams, and why many individuals, whether or not they are religious, who have paid particular attention to their "dream life," have discovered this "alertfulness" curiously instructive, strangely healing, and spiritually beneficial.

Treasures of the darkness

Working with our dreams, be they pleasant or troubling, as well as practicing the art of turning our night time wakefulness into "mindfulness," can provide rich opportunities for our spiritual development. It's not for nothing that we read in the Hebrew Scriptures: *"I will give you the treasures of the darkness"* (Isaiah 45:3). While a persistent inability to sleep requires proper medical attention and advice, the creative use of periodic bouts of night time sleeplessness may just prove to be the start of a life-changing spiritual adventure: if we are willing to work with them. (See the section on "Spiritual Drink")

What is your own experience?

- Are you a night owl – or an early bird? What is your favorite time of day?
- How would you describe your own night time routines and your sleep pattern?
- What is your "dream life" like?

Try these recipes

If you are continually waking up feeling exhausted then have a think about your work-life balance and your sleeping habits. Try the effects of a late evening bath or shower: warm, but not too hot or cold. Take advice if necessary.

Go for a week or two without having too many heavy or spicy late-night meals, alcoholic, or energy drinks, or having too much visual, mental, or intellectual stimulation in the evenings. See what happens.

Try this alternative midnight snack. When you visualize the point of light, as in the exercise above, let yourself move towards the light by rising up, or descending down, to it. See what happens on the journey. It's often much better than counting sheep!

Have a go at working with your dreams by making a note of them on paper as soon as you can. Then try to imagine or think what they might mean. Just let a meaning arise unbidden. The first interpretation will frequently be the "right one," though don't over-analyze it too much. Be open to the oddest of thoughts. What surfaces is normally more likely to be trivial, than it is momentous. But if something concerns you, then share it with a trusted friend or advisor.

Spiritual Snacks and Energy Drinks

Whatever food we like to eat, and whether or not we enjoy cooking for ourselves or our friends, our lifestyles often prevent us from taking adequate time to really enjoy our food. Texture and appearance, to say nothing of flavor and taste, are often entirely sacrificed in our rush to consume what's on the plate and move quickly on to the next item on our daily schedule.

A tip from the French

We need to learn to take time to relish our food: for the business of eating is about more than just what we consume. Food is meant to be a pleasure and a delight, *for our souls and spirits*, as much as for our eyes, minds, and stomachs.

Something of this can be savored in the difference between the two French words for food: "nourriture" and "cuisine." The first word simply means "nourishment:" all we need to consume in order to live. And it's often used by the French to describe English and American cooking, or else what's fed to animals! The word "cuisine," on the other hand, suggests careful preparation, beautiful presentation, mouth-watering tastes, *and the time to really enjoy it*, alone or with others. But it's important to remember that even the simplest and most ordinary of foods can equally be bliss to enjoy if we choose to make it so.

Take your time!
Just as we must learn to slow down or stop from time to time if we want to really enjoy being alive, taking our time to really experience our food is absolutely essential. From the moment we decide what to eat and begin to prepare our food, through the process of ensuring it's properly and appropriately cooked, to when we sit down to eat – pausing occasionally if we want to avoid indigestion – so the business of eating is not, as many of us have come to believe, all about "fast food." Good food takes time. For food is a deeply spiritual matter.

Spiritual snacks and energy drinks

Yet if we are people who find ourselves needing "food to go," or who frequently rely on those high power snacks or energy drinks to "keep us going" at times of stress, depression, elation, or adrenalin rush, then the following may be helpful.

For the equivalent of these high energy foods are those regular periods of "time out" for stillness, silence, and reconnection with our inner thoughts, feelings, and the "spirit within us," that are an essential dimension of good spirituality. Some people call these disciplines "mindfulness," as we have seen, while others may talk of "practicing the present moment," "being fully present," or "living in the here-and-now." Whatever we choose to call them they are in reality "spiritual snacks and energy drinks," serving the same function for our souls and spirits as their more familiar brand-name counterparts.

Taking five minutes break between activities works in a similar way. For just as eating healthy food allows the slow release of energy throughout the day, so "spiritual snacks and energy drinks" can boost our ability to focus on what really matters, on our interactions with others, and on our sense of connection to our human family and the world about us. Such "mindfulness" will also help us to spend some time each day being really conscious of the present moment, and alert to the way life actually is. Through these practices we can gain extraordinary insight into ourselves, into what makes us "tick," and into what's important about the issues we are immersed in at any one time. As well as receiving a deeper sense of our own meaning, value, and identity in relation to the universe of which we are a part.

This as true for "introverts" who get their energy from within, as it is for "extroverts" who recharge their batteries from the people and the world around them.

Discovering a taste for something else

Such moments of deep silence and stillness are also very close to aspects of what for many people can be called "prayer." For prayer, as we shall see later, is actually far more than the stereotypical "asking God for something" that many of us may have known and outgrown, just as we outgrew our belief in Father Christmas or Santa Claus.

Spiritual snacks and energy drinks help us to explore and nurture our ability to "take time out" for prayer, meditation, or contemplation: time for becoming alert or mindful of the present moment and for seeing the world differently as a result. They encourage ways of aiding our spiritual digestion and health, and allow our soul, spirit, or heart (call it what you will) to "ferment," to bubble up with an experience of "something else" that will potentially change and transform us for good.

The mysterious art of soul food

For just as cookery is about the skill of using ingredients, recipes, and the power of fire to change raw produce into "magical" food that will nourish, sustain, and delight us, so the art of soul feeding is about using the power of the spirit within us and around us to transform our whole sense of identity, being, and purpose. Through the use of readily available spiritual ingredients and techniques, it becomes possible to absorb, digest, and recreate an entirely new set of personal, social, and political priorities that will enable us to live life with a different understanding and practice of what it means for each of us to be fully human within the global family. That is spirituality at work!

What is your own experience?
- What are the kinds of things you usually eat and drink?
- What's your experience of silence and stillness?
- What is the most "spiritual" thing that has happened to you? What has moved you profoundly?
- What are your current priorities for living?

Try these recipes
- Make yourself a "spiritual snack" or mix yourself an "energy drink." See what happens.
- Have you ever wanted to experience a "taste for something else"? What might that be for you?
- If there were something you could change by the "power of prayer," what would it be?
- Take some time to be silent, still, or "prayerful" – or whatever you choose to call it. Try to use this time to imagine someone, or some situation, from a different perspective.
- Write a "soul recipe" for yourself. Take a selection of your hopes and fears, your high and low points, and mix them together by listing them on paper. Read aloud what you've written. When you're ready, write a sentence or a poem about the things you've listed. Or use paint or pencil. Or music or song. Use your body in movement or dance to express your feelings. Or else mull your thoughts over during a walk, jog, swim, or long bath. See what sort of soul nourishment results. Let its taste linger on your lips and in your heart for a while before deciding what to do next.

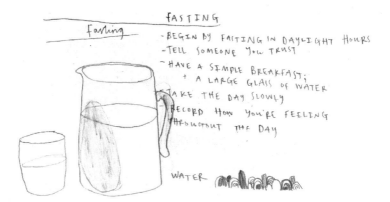

FASTING
- BEGIN BY FASTING IN DAYLIGHT HOURS
- TELL SOMEONE YOU TRUST
- HAVE A SIMPLE BREAKFAST;
  + A LARGE GLASS OF WATER
- TAKE THE DAY SLOWLY
- RECORD HOW YOU'RE FEELING
  THROUGHOUT THE DAY

WATER

Fasting

Going without

Frequently it seems that the very idea of "going without" or "doing without" has become something of an outrageous blasphemy for those of us living the West. An affront to our cherished lifestyles!

We are so completely used to being able to go into our local supermarket and find anything that our hearts may desire. As a matter of course we expect to find the shelves groaning with fresh food from the four corners of the world, a mind-boggling assortment of ready-made frozen dishes, a hundred varieties of ice-creams, and every known brand of bottled drink and confection. We take every opportunity for panic buying, stuffing our larders and fridges with the perishable goods we imagine we might urgently require to get us over the "lean times" of a public holiday. And this demand is readily reinforced by the policy of the supermarkets that there should be "no gaps" on their shelves that might deny the illusion of plenty, or give customers the impression that their store is failing to "satisfy our every need."

"Food in due season"

The idea of having "food in due season" (Psalms 145:15 and 104:27) seems so old fashioned these days. That there is a "proper time" for harvesting apples, or eating strawberries, or growing roses, goes against the grain of our expectations. For we have come to anticipate that anything and everything is there on demand in a nearby store. And the ease of transportation in today's global village seems well able to satisfy that belief.

Except of course that this ready flow of food and other goods is generally *all is one direction*: into the West. We rarely get to grips with the issue of the lack of political will to distribute and share food and resources with those in the "two-thirds" or "majority" world, who are genuinely going without and living well below what our Western life-style would consider to be the breadline.

Reclaiming the fast

The experience of fasting – of going without and being hungry – is one we urgently need to explore again as our ancestors did. For learning to fast might bring us to a greater appreciation, not only of our own real needs, but of those of people across the globe for whom hunger and want are routine realities.

While in many cultures fasting was – and is still – often regarded as a form of therapy for various mental and physical conditions, it has historically been seen primarily as a religious discipline. Abstinence from food, drink, sexual activity – refraining from "carnal" pleasures and excess – is a way of demonstrating or asserting our will power over our bodily needs. Often fasting is practiced in preparation for a particular festival, in honor of an event, a holy person, or as an act of penitence. Hence the great fasts of Ramadan, Yom Kippur, Advent, and Lent. Although it is clear that for many Christians, at least, fasting has become reduced to its blandest and most vestigial form in the giving up of chocolate, alcohol, or some other small symbolic act of self-denial.

A spiritual discipline

Fasting is first and foremost a *chosen act of spiritual discipline*. It's about limiting or denying ourselves food and drink. But is not a form of dieting, and will not serve that purpose.

Sometimes a fast is made during the daylight hours, sometimes more extensively: for shorter or for longer periods. To talk to anyone who fasts is to discover that, while it brings a liberating feeling of refreshment and exhilaration, it's also immensely hard work, very tiring, and demanding a radically altered approach to the pace of life.

It's also true is that metabolic change occurs during fasting. Often a restricted ability to concentrate for long periods, dizziness, and blackouts may be experienced as blood sugar levels are affected. So fasting should never be undertaken by those who have major or chronic medical conditions.

Very prolonged and rigorous fasting is also likely to cause hallucinations and altered states of mind, visions, or trances. And there is a mass of evidence to show that many people have understood these physiological effects as "mystical" experiences that have quite literally changed the direction of their lives. But, as we saw earlier with the interpretation of our dreams, whether or not we choose to ascribe these experiences to some divine cause, it's evident that new discoveries, fresh perspectives, and creative insights about ourselves and our spiritual journey may be had from the experience of fasting.

A new lifestyle

The experience of fasting may also serve another purpose. Those who fast will know that each fast must be "broken" by the consumption of a modest amount of food to avoid "crashing," or overloading, the digestive system after a period of inactivity. A little water and fruit is ideal for this.

In the same way, the decision to fast may be the trigger to opt for a simpler diet and a less complicated, more "ethically rich" lifestyle. Learning how to fast, how to "go without," is a great opportunity to decide against junk food, and highly processed and packaged meals, and to opt instead for locally sourced, simpler, healthier, and often cheaper food.

Fasting will also reward us with a sense of greater solidarity with the plight of many people in the world who have much less food and fewer life-style options than we do. And with so many groups and campaigns around it's now really easy to get involved in issues of global social justice. The real question for each of us is whether or not we can dare ourselves to explore what is a real opportunity for spiritual growth, and a chance to make a positive and lasting difference to the world.

What is your own experience?

- When did you last "go without"? What did this involve?
- Have you ever experienced hunger? What was it like?
- What combination of fresh and pre-cooked foods figure in your shopping?
- What is your involvement with the "politics" of food?

Try these recipes

- On your next shopping expedition make an effort to buy only those things that are locally sourced. Avoid buying things from the other side of the world or that are highly processed and over-packaged.
- Find out from a local greengrocer or gardener what's in season, and choose only those things to eat. Try to live seasonally for a year and see what difference it makes to your thinking – and to your finances!
- Learn to cook a simple soup. It's incredibly easy. First make the "base." Peel a potato the size of your fist and a skin a medium sized onion. Chop it all up and simmer it for ten minutes in a pan with half a pint of boiling water until it

goes soft and begins to disintegrate. Throw in a stock cube if you have one – but it's not that critical. *This mixture is the basic formula for any soup.* Then take whatever vegetables you've got in the amount you need. Chop them up into whatever size fits your spoon. Throw everything in and add extra water, until you think you've got enough liquid for your soup – thinner or thicker according to your taste. (A handful of dried lentils or some barley is great for thickening if it's too thin.) Again let it simmer until you have the consistency you want. Add a little seasoning. Whether or not you have a blender, you now have your very own soup – and the rest of your life to experiment with different recipes!

- Now if you want to fast ... First tell someone you trust that you're going to do it. Try it initially just for the daylight hours of one day. Start early with a simple but nourishing breakfast. A glass of tea or fruit juice and a bowl of unprocessed cereal of the "muesli" type (a combination of uncooked oats, fruit, and nuts) that will provide slow-release energy. You can even make your own secret recipe! Drink a large glass of water. Aim to have a quieter day than usual and don't do anything energetic. Take things slowly. When you feel hungry at the middle of the day go for a slow walk, try a "mindfulness" exercise, or read something interesting. You may also want to think about those for whom hunger is a normal part of everyday life. If you need a few sips of water now is the time to do so – especially if it's warm weather – but see if you can manage without. When dusk has arrived have some water and a piece of fruit. Take time to consume these slowly. Really notice their taste and texture and the *feeling* of what it is to take this food into your body.

- If you decide to fast for longer periods try to do so first at a time when you have more leisure than work. Perhaps over a weekend or during a vacation. Set sensible boundaries – daylight hours only initially, taking water if you really need to, and eating sensibly after the fast. Be alert to what is happening to you. Taking regular notes will be useful when it comes to reflecting on your experience and to discerning whether, and how, the fast has been of any spiritual benefit.

- Decide whether or not you need to simplify your life-style. Make an action plan and review it with a trusted friend after an agreed period.

- Get involved with a group or campaign that works for the fair distribution of food and resources, or for the relief of poverty. Let those who have less than you share their wisdom with you. See how it affects your life.

Feasting

Holy food

The word "feast" comes to us directly from the Latin "festum" which was a solemn religious event often accompanied by the consumption of food offered in sacrifice. This link between food and religious devotion has always been a strong one. While the Classical philosophers Epicurus, Pythagoras, and Socrates were all either vegetarians, or strongly advocated restraint from eating meat – as modern Hinduism and Jainism – animal sacrifice is closely associated with the origins and practice of other world religions. Indeed "food laws" and dietary restrictions play an important part of the religious observance and spiritual practice of many people today.

Mass catering

The American comedian Woody Allen is said to have remarked that the Bible "seems mostly about mass catering," and to some extent this is indeed true. There are lots of stories about people sharing food, about feeding and, of course, about cooking. And while the origins of human society are thought to be in part closely related to the practice of sharing and cooking of food killed or gathered communally, still today there are strong religious and social connotations to the business of eating together.

At the heart of every religious community there is the practice of *companionship:* a word that suggests more than its original narrow meaning of "sharing bread" (Latin "com" and "panis") with close friends and family. For the act of breaking bread and sharing food together symbolizes the forgiveness of any wrong doing or bad feeling and the restoration of "right relationships," peaceful co-existence, and equality in the community. And including strangers and "outsiders" in this action signifies the willingness to transcend the "outer limits" of friendship and mutuality, and extend the boundaries of inclusive community.

Celebration

While there are, sadly, divided communities across the world where sharing food and eating together remains an impossible and dangerous practice, for the majority of us it is a daily event of routine and unrecognized significance. One which we take so much for granted.

Yet at the same time, bizarrely, there is also a sense in which, despite our eagerness to find any excuse to attend or throw a party, and share food and drink with our friends and acquaintances, we remain in real danger of losing the true art of celebration.

Throwing a party is great fun. Deciding together who to invite, what music to play, what to eat and drink, and how to decorate the room, all serve to heighten the anticipation of the great day itself. This is just as true when planning "potluck dinners" (U.S.) and "faith suppers" (U.K.) where anyone might turn up and the guests themselves are trusted to bring food and drink to share! After all, does it really matter if not everything goes exactly to plan as long as we have a really good time?

Party time for the soul

But every day could be a celebration if we choose to make it so. For there's always *something* to celebrate!

Now this doesn't mean that we should be walking around with false grins on our faces. But it does suggest that we could take some of the best elements of a great party and use them to cultivate a "habit" of celebration. That we could learn in our daily lives how to be open to spontaneity and to the unexpected, so as not to be annoyed when "interruptions" occur to our schedules and our plans go awry. That we could learn to relax more, "chill," and not allow ourselves to get so stressed by things. That we could come to see the unfolding of the events of each day as the same kind of dynamic process and "gracious" interaction that happens when we give and receive gifts – even the "gift" of a smile or greeting. And, finally, that we should consciously treat the people we meet in the same unconditional way as we welcome guests at our party.

A "Kin-dom" recipe in the making

Learning how to celebrate "each day as it comes" for its unique and never-to-be-repeated interplay of events, encounters, insights, and creative possibilities is all about learning to see the world – and life itself – in a different way.

It's in this sense that Christians often talk of a "kingdom ethic," of a new perception of reality that comes when God, the "spirit of the divine," is recognized as being at work "reshaping" the world. But what people often fail to realize, however, is that the "g" is best understood as silent, unpronounced, and that, far from instigating a hierarchical "kingdom," the intended social order is intensely and urgently relational. It's all about "kin-dom."

For the discovery that all people are "kin," that everyone is ultimately related as brother and sister, and that humanity is one big global family, is surely the stunning and vital revelation of this new century. And with it comes the realization that we can no longer shun or escape the reality that, just as all people are called to experience and celebrate "life in all its fullness," so each of us is called to ensure that all people are invited to the feast. This is the end to which we must work, and the task to which we must commit ourselves.

Yes - the world needs to party more. So let's get busy making sure that everyone is invited, and that there's enough for all to share!

What is your own experience?

- When, what, and where did you last really celebrate something? What was it like?
- Are you a "party animal," or does the thought of being in a crowd leave you feeling drained?
- What would your own "ideal" party be like, and who would be the guests?
- What are the most memorable "moments" of your life so far? What is it about them that makes them so unforgettable and worth celebrating?

Try these recipes

- Prepare a feast for yourself and your friends. It can take any form you like, but take time to make special "holy" food. Prepare it from ingredients that are as fresh or as little processed as possible. Create a special ambiance or setting for your meal. Light a few candles or decorate the space in some seasonal way. Welcome your friends by name and make it a very special time of sharing.
- Join the party at your local homeless center or drop-in. Try to discover what this experience can teach you about feasting and celebration.
- Begin to prepare a list of your own "kin-dom" recipes to delight your soul. It could take the form of a regime, action plan, or "rule of life" (see "Recipes for Sharing"). It will help you to describe your own aliveness, to celebrate the

relationships you have, the gifts and skills you have been given, and the things you have to share with others, and to explore your connections to the people with whom you share this planet.

Al Fresco Food: Picnics and Pilgrimages

"Then people long to go on pilgrimages"

Long before tourism was invented, people with time and money to spare would go on a pilgrimage. The purpose was supposedly wholly devotional. To visit the shrine, birth, or burial place of a saint or holy person; generally with a view to obtaining some religious benefit or merit for this life or in the next. In reality the opportunity for adventure and stories, and new places and faces, was often an equal or even greater attraction!

Pilgrimage was, however, always a risky business, even in the company of others. Going beyond one's own territory and boundaries, leaving behind the security of local knowledge and "know how," and "traveling through the countryside like a stranger" (which is what the word "pilgrim" originally meant) was inevitably fraught with dangers: highway robbery, murder, and abduction, to say nothing of being taken advantage of at every turn in taverns and market places.

Finding the way

There were, of course, no "maps" – since the precise objective knowledge of an area that maps contain wasn't possible until very recently – and the charts that the very rich might on occasion have had, plotted only relative position, and gave only vague directions and general ideas of what landmarks to look out for on the way. Consequently the "journey" was literally a "day-to-day" progression, moving from one evening lodging place to the next, and relying on local guidance and information.

Moving to a different rhythm

Anyone who's been on vacation or holiday will know that when the pressures of daily living fall away, life seems to move at a slower pace. We are able to take our time, linger over things, and loiter awhile doing nothing in particular. The very word "saunter" (from the French "sainte terre") derives from the consciousness of a new way of being and behaving that is experienced when we cross over the threshold into "holy ground" and begin to move through it in a different way.

This new rhythm is explicitly explored in the Zen Buddhist practice of "kinhin." This is a form of walking meditation in which the mind is concentrated on the deliberate placing of one foot slowly in front of another after each breath. Here walking ceases to be a means of moving between places and becomes, instead, an act of "mindfulness" where the attention is focused on peeling back the layers of consciousness, and on being entirely alert to the nature of human identity: to become fully alive in the present moment.

Eating in the open air

Being outdoors in the fresh air also seems to sharpen our appetite, and make the food we eat appear to taste so much better, giving it extra flavor and improved texture and appearance. So whether we have a picnic on the grass, a barbecue by the beach, or a simple packed lunch by the wayside, the very act of being outside our usual environment serves to heighten our senses.

Something of this resonates with the idea of journeying and pilgrimage, where the experience of traveling into unknown places has the potential not only to affect our senses but to change our attitudes and give us appetites for different things. For just as the process of traveling may cause us to experience different sorts of foods, tastes, and smells, so we may find ourselves discovering new interests, and unexpected enthusiasms for all kinds of odd things.

Returning home a changed person

It is well-known that medieval "maps" and ancient sea charts commonly contain drawings of monsters and ferocious hybrid animals with the words "here be dragons" at the edges of the paper, or in those places beyond the frontiers of human knowledge, where no-one had hitherto ventured. Indeed the idea of the "monster" was – and still is – a symbol of the limits of human ability to understand and explain, and of the fear of all that lies outside our knowledge or experience.

One of the ritual functions of pilgrimage was the idea that the sheer effort of making the journey, and the experience of encountering "the unknown," or "the divine," on "holy ground," would ensure that the pilgrim returned home a different person.

In the same way today, pilgrimage, voyaging into the "great outdoors," stepping outside of all that is safe and familiar to us, and crossing the threshold of our experience, can still serve as a mechanism that allows us to face those real and imaginary fears and dangers that we routinely suppose threaten our identity, security, and existence. Daring ourselves to take set off into the unknown with only those few provisions we can readily carry is a powerful way for us to blow away the stale air that stunts our spiritual growth and allow ourselves to be refreshed in body, mind, and soul.

What is your own experience?

- What are your experiences and memories of outdoor meals? Spend some time recalling these.
- What things has travel taught you about yourself?
- What would be your fears and insecurities about being alone in an unknown place?

Try these recipes

- Go on a journey to a place you've never visited. It needn't be too far away, because you're going to go on foot and take with you only those provisions – food, drink, clothing, and shelter that you can carry. You are not permitted to take a map or a compass, and the use of phones as directional aids is strictly forbidden – though you may take photos on the journey! Try to travel only by your own inner sense of direction, by following the sun (or the moon and stars!) or local landmarks, and by asking people the way. As you go, make your own chart and keep a log of all that happens. Pay particular attention to the process of walking and breathing. Notice the rhythms. See where your thoughts and feelings take you. And remember that the journey from your head to your heart is often longer and more arduous that the physical route and distance you travel.
- Try to make a "walking meditation." It's best to do it just around your garden, backyard, or other enclosed space – and do it in a circle. That way you don't have to think too much about the direction. Set yourself thirty minutes or an hour for this. Again, the task is to pay particular attention to the rhythm of your walking and breathing. Try to "rise above" your thoughts and feelings by concentrating solely

on being in the present moment. Do nothing else but breath and walk. If your minds strays (as it will!) bring it gently back to the process.

- Take some food to eat it in a quiet spot outside. The weather is irrelevant – just dress appropriately! Concentrate on your awareness of your senses and on the process of eating. Consume your food slowly. Be aware of each mouthful as it enters your body, even trying to track its progress into your stomach. See what you learn from the experience and from being out in the open.

- Go and visit a shrine, holy place, or sacred spot. You may use the journey recipe again – or just make the visit and spend an hour or two at your destination. Simply observe what happens and what your thoughts and feelings are.

- Make your own shrine, holy place, or sacred spot in a favorite location. Use your imagination to structure it in any way you choose. Spend some time there as often as possible.

Spiritual Drink

Gladdening the heart or deadening the soul?

The use of alcohol, along with drugs and tobacco, is a contested issue for many religions. Consequently, while its use is prohibited by some faiths, most others are alert to its potential for both good and for ill. So we can find in the Hebrew Scriptures nuggets of wisdom like: "Wine drunk at the proper time and in moderation is rejoicing of heart and gladness of soul" (Ecclesiasticus 31:28), and conversely: "Do not try to prove your strength by wine-drinking" (Ecclesiasticus 31:25). We will all have our own experiences to share.

Being hung over

Most of us are also aware of the consequences of over-indulgence. Not only the ability of these substances to loosen both our inhibitions and our grip on reality, but also to have effects the following day in various forms of painful withdrawal or hangover. While hangovers are usually experienced the morning after, they can occur anytime and cause not only physical effects such as headaches, nausea, and sensitivity to noise and light, but they can also trigger or exacerbate feelings of anxiety and depression. And while a magic potion to cure these ill effects is still eagerly awaited, generally speaking rehydration of the body by drinking water before sleeping is a very good place to start.

A bit like life itself

Now most people probably knew that already. Less well known is that life itself can sometimes leave us feeling hung over. While this may be due to a variety of external forces beyond our control, or to the surfacing of unspoken fears and doubts from within, the absence of a satisfying and meaningful spiritual life can also cause us to experience similar sensations to a hangover. For often when life "gets too much" for us, or loses its "sparkle," when nothing seems to go right, or the future seems hopeless and we feel frustrated at every turn, the underlying issue may, to be surprising extent, also prove to be a spiritual one.

Dark night of the soul

For centuries people who have given their entire lives to prayer, meditation, or contemplation, and to living as devout and holy a life as possible, have experienced times of frustrating "spiritual dryness," when the lights go out for them and they feel utterly left in the dark. Such times are often described as a "dark night of the soul." Accounts of this phenomenon use language that ranges from talk of "simply nothing seems to happen when I pray or meditate," to "when I think about my life, I just can't imagine a way forward," through to "I see or feel only darkness around me," or "despite all my efforts I only feel dryness and despair."

So what to do?

Such thoughts and feelings are not at all uncommon to anyone who is trying to take their spiritual life seriously. And the truth is that there is usually no telling how long such a situation might last. In a way these experiences are the spiritual equivalent of the chill we feel when the sun goes behind a cloud and is hidden from sight. As a result they are often termed experiences of "*de*solation," and contrasted to times when the sun comes out and we feel joyful: "*con*solation."

There are two very important responses we need to make to

this situation. The first is to talk with someone we trust and respect for their commitment to traveling their own spiritual path. It's so very important that we learn from those whose journey may likely have taken them through similar experiences. It's also important that we have someone close by who is able to keep an eye out for things we may not always notice: particularly the interaction between our spiritual, mental, and physical health.

The second response is to learn patience. Most of the greatest mystics and spiritual gurus have at some point in their journey found themselves in this same place, and they are all of the same opinion: that the best thing to do is simply to remain faithful to the spiritual quest and not to give up. For learning to wait, patiently and unafraid, in the darkness without being either panicked or seduced by the need for a sense of "progress," "success," or "achievement," is indeed the beginning of spiritual insight and wisdom.

Drinking deep from our own spiritual wells

Living in the West we are not used to droughts of any kind. We slip naturally and inevitably into the expectation that there is always plenty to drink. So we are not very patient and not used to having to wait for anything. Yet just as wine and beer need time to ferment before they become mature and full-bodied enough to drink and enjoy, so we need time and patient effort to develop a full-bodied spiritual life. This spiritual maturation requires that we persevere with the task of awaiting the natural end of episodes of spiritual dryness, darkness, and dysfunction: until something new emerges. As it will.

It may of course be that, in time, the build up of pressure from deep within our being will force its way through to the surface in some sort of "crisis." (See "Comfort Eating.") It may be that conversation with a trusted other, or our self-expression through our creativity, or physical exercise, or playful activity, will loosen the blockage and allow the life-giving energy to flow. The point is not to try to take deliberate short-cuts, or to bring the process to an unnatural or premature conclusion.

Time and again the experience of those who take seriously the demands and opportunities of exploring the spiritual life has demonstrated that when we place ourselves in a relationship of *intentional openness* to "the Other," to "otherness," or "to what-is-not-yet-us" then extraordinary things can happen. We find ourselves experiencing the life-changing energy that sustains the universe.

Spiritual thirst quenching

This deliberate opening ourselves and seeking to connect with "otherness" and to the mystery of the universe that surrounds us and that manifests itself in people and in creation – the mystery that some call "God" – is a process that many people call prayer, or meditation and contemplation. All religions advocate and practice this process, and there is an immense amount of interest in those religions known for using the language of meditation and contemplation: Buddhism, Taoism, Islamic Sufism, and so on. And there are similarly rich traditions to explore within Judaism and Christianity, although these are all too often overlooked.

Above all it's important to remember that meditation and prayer are not the sole preserve of the religious. They are there for all people to use and to adapt to their own needs.

The challenge is to realize that prayer is infinitely more than the idea of asking favors from an all-powerful "being in the sky." Prayer, like meditation and contemplation, is fundamentally about connecting to the creative energy – call it "divine" if you wish – that is flowing through all of creation. But the extraordinary thing is that, whether or not we believe in God, as we seek to put ourselves in touch with this energy, it can very often *feel* as though it's relational. It can feel like we're in touch with another living "personality."

Now this is a highly subjective statement that's impossible to substantiate. It may simply be the result of the way our minds work. Either way, it's really not that significant to the end result. What is important is to realize that the practice of prayer, meditation, and contemplation are integral dimensions to our spiritual development. We should try them out and see what difference it makes.

What is your own experience?

- What are your own stories about over-indulgence?
- Does the language of "dark night of the soul" and "spiritual thirst" have any meaning for you?
- What is your experience of prayer, meditation, or contemplation?

Try these recipes

- Try this meditation. Sit comfortably and in an upright posture, with your hands on your lap and your eyes closed. Become aware of your breathing, but do not alter its rhythm. Notice the cold air as it enters your nostrils and the warm air as it leaves them. Focus your whole attention on this activity. If there are distracting noises nearby, simply name them: "bird," "aircraft" etc. Let them go and return to your breathing. Likewise if you have any distracting thoughts, don't follow them, just keep focused on the breathing. If the distractions continue it may help to use a "mantra." This is a word or short phrase repeated slowly over again in your head. Any word or phrase will do, but many people like to choose something meaningful or unique to them alone. It may be of religious significance: "Jesus," "Maranatha," "Allahu Akbar," or "Om," or else it may be a word such as "peace," or "love." Its function is simply to give your mind something to focus on while you meditate. Similarly you may opt to focus on a candle flame or an image for the same reason.

• The task is simply to do the work of meditation, to say the mantra over and over. Thirty minutes of meditation morning and evening can bring real benefits. It can teach us discernment, to "notice" the way our minds operate and the subtle tendencies of thought, habit, and action that can have a negative influence on our spiritual development. It's important though to remember that while patient commitment to the practice is required, we mustn't be too hard on ourselves when we fail. We must simply begin again.

• Remembering what we said about personality types, you may prefer to try this different meditation which uses a more imaginative approach.

Step One: Close your eyes and imagine yourself leaving your room and going into a garden. Perhaps one you know, or have visited, perhaps not. In your mind's eye walk around this garden and see what can be seen: flowers, trees, grass. Stay with this picture for a while …

Step Two: As you walk around the garden you come to a grapevine – supported on a trellis, wire, or wall. Go up and have a good look at it. Notice the strong, gnarled, twisted trunk and how all the branches, and leaves are supported by it. Have a good look at that trunk, its texture, bark, the shapes it makes, its color. Stay with this picture for a while ...

Step Three: Suddenly you become aware of someone next to you. It's the gardener who, proud of his vine, wants to explain it all to you. He touches the trunk, branches, leaves, and the fruit. Look closely at the fruit, how delicious it looks. Try a grape. Taste it how good it is. Stay with this picture for a while ...

Step Four: The gardener asks what fruit you would like to grow in your life. Think about this for a while. Then respond. Ask for any help you need to live a fruitful life. When you're ready, come back into the present moment.

- Here's a very personal meditation for those times when you feel low. Make yourself comfortable in a favourite place. You may like to start by using the breathing exercise from the first meditation. Then, aloud or silently, say the words: "I like myself because I am good enough." "I like myself because I am good enough." Now each of the words of this simple phrase may be stressed differently. So that there are, in fact, eight separate ways of saying the whole sentence. Try each of the variations in turn and see which one you most like. Which one best resonates with your feelings? Which one most encourages your smile?

Take your time. Say the words slowly. With each inhalation draw the words down into your body. Let their astonishing power begin to work their magic: loosening the knots of discontent and self-dislike that limit your capacity to embrace yourself, warts and all. "I like myself because I am good *enough*." "I like myself because *I am* good enough." And when you're ready, end by daring yourself to say aloud: "I choose to like myself. I actually like myself."

- If you feel nothing is happening when you meditate or practice mindfulness, then consider this. If we decide to open ourselves in this way, we shouldn't be surprised if it sometimes feels hard-going, "dry," and unproductive. Most people pray or meditate to find inner harmony, calm, love, joy, or connection – or else answers and outcomes. But the process takes time and it's vital we try not to get disheartened! When we come face to face with our spiritual "dryness," or else feel overwhelmed with negative thoughts, it can seem that there's an impossible mountain to climb. We might even feel like giving up altogether and letting despair fill us completely. Yet paradoxically these feelings of hard struggle could well be moments of "crisis": opportunities for growth and change, when we move from one sort of awareness of "God," "the divine," or "reality" to a different one, as we'll see in the next chapter. So it's best to try and stay with the process and to open ourselves to what lies ahead. Hold on to the fact that, while we may *feel* that the praying, meditating, or mindfulness is all "up to us," perhaps the best thing to do is just to stay where we are and let the process come to us. But, once again, you may get real benefit and support from speaking with someone who is also, like you, traveling the spiritual path, and from seeing what might come of that conversation.

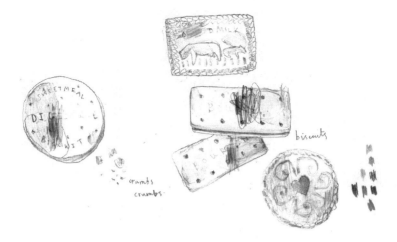

Comfort Eating

Natural instincts

When times are tough and our spirits are low, as they will inevitably be from time to time, then one of our most instinctual responses it to eat or drink. Whatever our particular "comfort" food, the underlying impulse is surely to recreate those times when, as infants, we were fed warm sweet milk safe in the arms of those who loved us unconditionally. This is possibly why, though any food can be comfort food, most people tend to prefer sweet, easily digestible things. And there's nothing wrong with that!

Just desserts and just deserts?

Many people simply adore desserts – the "afters," "pudding," or sweet course following a meal – and a few prefer to eat only dessert courses! For them it's "just desserts" all the time, whether or not they've finished or even had a main course and actually merit their "just deserts!"

Now this pun, beloved of restaurant owners everywhere, points to a subtle truth about ourselves. We are creatures of comfort. Just as we like our comfort food when times are hard, so we love to savor the sweet comforting taste of reward when our efforts are over and our work is done. We like to be contented and satisfied. But does that mean we're happy?

Living the discomfort

Some of us will do anything for an easy life and will avoid conflict and stress by staying well within our comfort zone. But there are enormous rewards and opportunities to be had by stepping outside whatever boxes we prefer to inhabit.

We saw in the previous chapter that the experience of spiritual struggle, "blockage," "dryness," and "darkness" may actually be signs of emerging "crises" or interim states of flux. When we prepare ourselves psychologically and spiritually to move – or be drawn – from one state of perception, understanding, or being to another. The word "crisis" comes from a Greek concept suggesting a "moment for decision." And so in reality, a "crisis" is much less about panic and chaos and much more about an occasion that is presenting itself to us: a "liminal" ("threshold" or "doorway") time between two stages of our life.

Consequently when crises occur we should take seriously the opportunity they present for change and growth. And we should try to find within ourselves the reserves of curiosity, courage, and determination to ride the feelings of anxiety and dread that can carry us over, across the horizon that is beckoning, to explore what lies beyond.

Moving into a new place

Crossing horizons, boundaries, and frontiers, as we saw earlier, invites encounters with new concepts and ideas, and with "otherness" and "difference." And if we want to see the world through new eyes, we have to leave behind all kinds of baggage that we are carrying from our earlier life. This can frequently be painful, uncomfortable, and *rarely ever risk-free*.

Yet this is precisely how the world is. Just as the universe is continuously evolving, so human thought responds by similarly adapting: moving from model to model, hypothesis to hypothesis.

And though religion and spirituality may be deeply rooted in ancient wisdom and practices, they never operate in a timeless vacuum. How ever much we may be influenced by the past, we are always people of the present time and our religious and spiritual practices function – or not – in the present moment. So it is that, similarly, our quest for "God," for "things of the spirit," for "religious meaning" must *begin* in the here and now and in those ideas, events, and intuitions that are on the "dangerous edge of things," but then *be oriented towards* those future disclosures and revelations that are being birthed all around us.

Discovering new tastes and flavors

The word "comfort" was originally associated with strength, bravery, courage, and support: the kinds of virtues that were needed when the going got tough. So "comfort food" would have had very different connotations for our ancestors who risked ocean crossings, desert treks, and bloody battlegrounds for the promise of a new life and new opportunities. And a similar challenge is there for us today.

The human family and the world we inhabit and share with the rest of creation needs people who are willing to be explorers. Scientists, economists, inventors, politicians, agriculturalists, and artists of all kinds are indispensable, to be sure. But, having been ill-served for too long by our religious groups and institutions, we have sought fulfillment and happiness in materialist, militaristic, and consumerist approaches to life. Now, more than ever before, Western societies *have a critical shortage of people willing be spiritual explorers.*

Now is the time to call forth those who are willing to set out and re-discover the vast spiritual soulscapes that were once so well-known, as well as exploring those that still lie uncharted.

People who are committed to helping mend the *dangerous tear* that has opened up in the canvas of human self-understanding, wisdom, and ethical action. People who are curious and brave enough to try out the extraordinary new tastes and flavors that await us. Just over the horizon.

What is your own experience?

- When do you need "comfort food" and what kinds of things do you consume?
- What is the particular box or comfort zone that you inhabit?
- What "crises" have you faced in your life?
- What happened when you last took a personal risk?

Try these recipes

- Look again at the chart of your spiritual journey that you made earlier (See "Travel"). Focus in particular on the space you left for your future adventures. What new steps have you taken since you made the chart that you can now include on it? Where are you up to on your journey? Can you identify those issues that are on your "growing" or "dangerous" edge: the boundary markers on the frontiers of your spiritual map, beyond which there may be "dragons?" What are the options you need to consider for moving forward? Or would you prefer to stay where you are? What, if anything, is holding you back? Be as honest as you can.
- Here's an old religious joke. "How do you make God laugh? Tell God your plans!" So, without attempting to plan or control the outcomes, consciously try to place yourself at your growing edge. Choose a few of the ideas or

practices we have already discussed that you have yet to try. Give them a go – and be open to whatever happens.

- Supposing you decide to explore your spirituality as openly as you can, how do you hope or imagine it might actually impact on you, in terms of what you want to do with your life? And how will others benefit?

- If you have not yet done so, then find someone you feel you can trust to discuss these issues with.

Coffee and Cake and a Quiet Chat

Meet Francis and Clare

There's a story that, once, their followers were busy searching for St Francis and St Clare in the middle of a dark forest. They were guided towards a strange light and found the two saints deep in "holy conversation," surrounded by a radiant glow apparently emanating from their hearts and souls!

Now there are many similar stories about spiritual adventurers in all of the world's religions, as well as comparable tales involving non-religious folk. Indeed such "meetings of minds" between friends is commonplace, and a random visit to a café will generally reveal lots of people absorbed in deep conversation over coffee and cake. For, as we have seen, friendship demands open, honest communication, and intimate conversation is at the heart of the human desire to relate.

Greeting one another

Much of this is encapsulated in the words of greeting used in different parts of the world. The Hebrew "Shalom" and Arabic "Salaam" both suggest a wish for peace, wholeness, well-being, or blessing. Likewise the Hawaiian "Aloha;" whereas the common Indian greeting "Namaste" can be rendered as "I greet the God within you" or, in a more philosophically "yogic" translation: "I honor in you that place where the Lord – or the Universe – resides. And when you are in that place in you, and I am in that place in me, then there is only one of us." So greeting another with a desire for that person's flourishing, and in recognition that "there is that of the Spirit/spirit in each of us," as the Quakers say, is to acknowledge that there is something extraordinary and eternal in all people that is worthy of being addressed, valued, and befriended.

Spiritual friendship

Spiritual relationships are encouraged by all the world's religions and cultures, whether it is between "gurus" and their adherents and followers, "masters" or "teachers" and their disciples, or "pastors" and members of their congregations. But because the issue of the power dynamic in these relationships has rightly been the subject of detailed scrutiny, it is always sensible to avoid those relationships that seem inappropriate, or in any way one-sided, or coercive. It's also worth remembering that any real spiritual teacher will not prevent someone from walking away when they wish to.

While in the West the language of "spiritual directors," "soul friends," or "prayer guides" has made a real come back, the essential qualities to look for when seeking a partner for our spiritual one-to-one conversations, is primarily someone who can be trusted to take seriously, non-judgmentally, and confidentially whatever we have to say, and to offer unconditional spiritual friendship and support to another individual on his or her own unique spiritual journey.

Soul talk

Such holy conversation is about honest, respectful sharing, and active, non-intrusive listening. It's about *creating space* for exploration and discernment, by one person being a kind of "mirror" or "sounding board" for another, reflecting back a person's own thoughts and feelings, doubts and desires. And perhaps thereby prompting or enabling that person to take whatever steps he or she needs to take towards or across his or her spiritual horizon.

It's about the non-directive sharing of mutual experiences of the spiritual life and the identification of those "triggers," "gestalts," or "aha! moments" that usher in new perceptions of self and others that in turn release fresh energy, commitment, and direction. It's about using conversation – and that's *not the same* as superficial banter or gossip – as a dialogical tool for identifying and potentially relinquishing familiar and simplistic patterns of thinking and behavior, and for discerning new possibilities for the performance of our life.

Spiritual intimacy

It's also the case that silence may be a sign and a product of this shared intimacy. For while the story of Francis and Clare has them deep in holy conversation, there are plenty of accounts of other people *simply sitting silently* in each other's presence. Just as a deep bond may develop between two individuals who have lived closely together or shared their lives over many years, whereby few if any words are needed or used in the relationship, so silence may be discovered to be an extraordinarily effective medium for deep knowing and intimate communication. For silence is frequently the manifestation of the spiritual attunement and harmony between people that has grown up in response to the long-term mutual giving and receiving of trust and attentiveness. At the same time, silence may also be the normal and natural reaction when we find ourselves in the presence of someone whom we feel instinctively has not only been on a spiritual journey, but has returned as the bearer of some profound insight that cannot be communicated with words and for which an awed but rich silence is the only appropriate medium.

The long and the short of it is that we should more readily explore and cultivate silence and learn to "rest in it" when it comes our way. That we should accustom ourselves to it, and get to a place where we don't allow the silence to embarrass or intimidate us into speaking – just for the sake of it. For it is so wonderfully liberating to be silent, alone or with another: to just be attentive and see what emerges.

What is your own experience?
- What are the best conversations you've had recently?
- What made them so memorable?
- When were the times that you have been aware of the amazing uniqueness of another person?
- What "aha! moments" have you experienced, when your understanding of something has been suddenly changed and new perceptions have arisen?
- What is your experience of silence?

Try these recipes
- Try to initiate a conversation about spiritual journeys with someone you trust. See where the conversation goes.
- Next time you find yourself with someone and a silence develops, see how long it can be maintained. When the silence is broken, try to have a conversation about the silence.
- At the end of your day, think back over the conversations you have had. Learn to distinguish between superficial banter or gossip and the really meaningful exchanges. Then try to apply this skill of discernment to other aspects of your life.
- Make a list of the qualities you think you have to offer someone as a "spiritual friend."
- Then make a list of the expectations you would have of someone who was to have this role for you. Be on the look

out for such a person and, when you find him or her, don't be afraid to ask. It is perfectly normal practice to enter into such a relationship, initially on a trial basis. Take two or three meetings before you decide whether or not to make a longer commitment. Most spiritual friendships are open-ended, but with the clear understanding from the outset that they can be dissolved by either party at any point, and that no-one will make a fuss or take offence.

Recycling the Left-overs

When things go wrong

Whether we have high hopes for a meal with friends, a piece of work, a new relationship or job, or our cherished aspirations for future success, sooner or later something will backfire. And at such times we just have to pick ourselves up, dust ourselves down, and start all over – or else sit alone licking our wounds at what someone once aptly called "a pity party." Of course things can go wrong for no particular reason. Often things are just out of our control. And sometimes things are entirely down to other people. But, from time to time, what goes wrong is entirely of our own making, and is solely our personal fault and responsibility. And on these occasions, what are we to do?

Well – we could pretend it wasn't our mistake and just walk away, denying responsibility. But, if we're honest with ourselves, we always know, deep down, when we're responsible. And there's really no point in trying to fool ourselves! For we can all be self-centered and just "plain selfish"; though it's often really quite difficult to stand up, admit responsibility, to ourselves and others – and take the consequences. After all no-one really relishes carrying blame and guilt, or owning up to causing pain and suffering for others, however trivial.

Recognizing the scale of the problem

Yet good spirituality is not just about admitting our imperfections and the error of our ways, but about having the maturity to take responsibility, apologize, and make amends. And we're not very good at that in our contemporary society. We just have to listen to the way many politicians and worlds leaders talk to see that this is so!

Having a healthy and robust spirituality requires us to have both the courage to deal with the issues, and the compassion to forgive ourselves, when we cause grief to others and to ourselves. And it's this self-forgiveness that is often the hardest and most painful thing of all. For the things we do wrong – whether we prefer to talk about our individual human shortcomings as innate selfishness, as natural human imperfection, or indeed as "sinfulness" – all too often leave us with a great deal of "toxic emotional waste" to dispose of.

Creative recycling

In the same way that we have become alert to the need for responsibly recycling the left-overs of our meals and the waste our homes and industries generate, so we need to strive to responsibly and creatively and effectively dispose of the harmful by-products of our own accidental errors and deliberate foolhardiness. Just as we now think twice about the contents of what we dump in our oceans or in landfill sites, so we need to think long and hard about the consequences of anonymously dumping our mistakes in conveniently concealed holes, mixing them up in layers of noxious guilt and lethal shame, and covering the whole lot with a thin veneer of respectable soil and turf!

Guilt and shame are two of the most destructive emotions we possess, and failure to deal with them effectively can easily lead to psychological and spiritual trauma. When we feel guilt for things we've done wrong, the solution is always to recognize our errors, say sorry, and try to avoid making the same mistake twice.

(And if we're feeling guilt for things that are not of our own causing, then we should make an urgent point of talking with someone we trust.) It's also essential to receive forgiveness, and here often the hardest thing of all, of course, is to forgive ourselves. However, while acknowledging guilt is one thing, dealing with shame is quite another.

For, unlike guilt, shame remains essentially hidden, deeply internalized, and generally unspoken or "unconfessed." For shame is bound up with those things about ourselves that we fear to tell anyone. Even though there is a sense in which feelings of shame serve to police the limits of appropriate personal behavior, shame is chronically destructive and can seriously prevent human flourishing. In this regard shame is allied to, and often engendered by, those religions which use the fear of being shamed to buttress their belief systems and maintain the boundaries of their community identity and conformity to ethical norms. Hence the dilemmas faced by many members of religious groups whose personal identity, beliefs, or lifestyle choices may be deemed to infringe the group's moral code, traditions, or expectations. We might think particularly of those for whom the fear of being discovered and shamed for being, say, gay, transgender, a single parent, a drug user, or an ex-offender, obliges them to live a double life and deny something fundamental about their own experience.

Organic transformation

Yet just as we have increasingly come to expect that all kinds of waste can – and should – be recycled, so it is possible to imagine that guilt and shame might also be transformed into something more useful.

Most, if not all, religions, spiritualities, and secular philosophies share the belief that individual and communal transformation is possible and desirable, and that wholeness and flourishing are legitimate human aspirations for everyone in the twenty-first century. And if that's so, then it's not unreasonable to expect that a more thoroughgoing and inclusive understanding of the complexity of human nature, and of the multiform practices of human behavior, *must emerge* from such groups. A theology that is finally capable of addressing the failure of so many religious groups to empower people to find the flourishing they desire and the wholeness that such groups are supposed to offer.

Perhaps the place to start is by radically unlearning our presuppositions about the nature of "the divine," the moral life, and the spiritual quest, and by starting over with *a more holistic and embodied practice* that enables people to reconnect organically with the transforming spirit of the divine within each one of us.

What is your own experience?

- How do you contribute to the recycling effort?
- What things have gone wrong for you in the past, and how did you respond?
- How do these ideas about shame resonate with you?
- What, if anything, would you wish to see transformed about you or your life?

Try these recipes

- Take some time to try the following exercises. Again your notebook will come in handy.
- Think of an occasion when you did something you later regretted. How did this make you feel at the time? How did you handle those feelings? At what point did you manage to let go of any feelings of regret or guilt? What caused you to be able to do this? Was it simply the passage of time, or acknowledging responsibility, or being able to

forgive yourself? Or was it something else altogether?

- Now think of an occasion when you did something regrettable that involved another person.

    How did you resolve this? Was it simply the passage of time, or acknowledging responsibility, or being able to forgive yourself? Or was it something else altogether?

- Is there something in your life which makes you feel ashamed or shameful? How might you let go of such feelings? Perhaps you could write down your feelings and then symbolically burn the paper. Or you may prefer to talk with someone confidentially.

- How might you express your concerns, anger, or pain about the harmful or exploitative actions of the big institutions, international corporations, and global structures of our world?

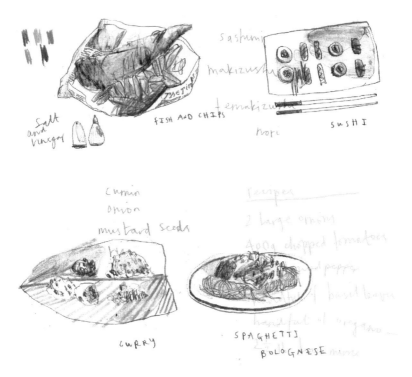

Salt and Vinegar

FISH AND CHIPS

Sashimi

makizushi

temakizu

nori

SUSHI

Cumin
Onion
mustard seeds

CURRY

recipes
2 large onions
400g chopped tomatoes
pepper
basil leaves
handful of oregano

SPAGHETTI BOLOGNESE

Dining Out – a Guide to Foreign Food

Finding somewhere to eat

These days there are so many places to eat out. And while the word "restaurant" originally referred to a kind of *restorative* hodgepodge, soup, or stew that was sold in many taverns to passing travelers, these days restaurants serve many kinds of specialist ethnic and local dishes. Indeed, in most towns and cities the restaurants are simply listed according to the "nationality" of the food they offer. So chances are, if you plan to eat out with friends, the question "where shall we eat?" will require an initial choice between several different national or ethnic cuisines.

Tasting the difference

Not only will the food be different according to its country of origin, but it will likely be the product of a whole range of religious and cultural beliefs and practices at every stage of its preparation. Jewish food will be kosher and Asian, North African, and Eastern Mediterranean will usually be halal – and both will have involved prayers as part of the ritual slaughter of the animals. Food made by Baha'i's and Jains will be vegetarian, as will most Hindu meals, though any meat dishes here will never contain beef. And restaurants will probably not sell alcoholic drinks if certain religious sensitivities are to be honored.

But in contrast to how things were even a generation ago, this taste for foreign food is something that is now almost entirely commonplace. Most of us have happily adapted our daily diet to accommodate a taste for the unusual and exotic. And on the culinary level, at least, we are very comfortable with the idea of difference. We happily choose unfamiliar dishes from the menu and try a wide range of new taste experiences. But this enthusiastic experimentation cannot, however, be taken for granted when it comes to our experience of religious and spiritual difference. For in this realm we have tended to remain contentedly within what is safe, familiar, and unchallenging.

Food that's out of our world

Yet soul making is precisely all about experimentation and about developing an interest in what's out of the ordinary and unusual. So perhaps the best way of expanding our spiritual horizons is to mix with people from different ethnic and religious backgrounds and learn to inhabit their world a little, so as to enrich our own.

For what's really important to remember is that while people may appear very different from each other, speak a language that's incomprehensible to an outsider, and have unfamiliar cultural habits, at the end of the day *people are just people*. While we may differ with regard to some aspects of our identity, there is a vast amount that we all have in common. Whatever our backgrounds, people are still either male or female, black or white, straight or gay, vegan, vegetarian, or meat-eaters, left- or right-handed, and with the same range of tastes in sport, music, politics, film, and everything else in between. And any differences we have on the level of our religious and spiritual practice will only represent a very small part of our human identity.

Recipes to try and food to share

Getting to know people whose religious world view is not the same as ours but may overlap with it to some extent, is a fantastic way of deepening our own knowledge and experience. It also enables us to better resist those pressures and tendencies across the world that seek to reduce people to a single identity which can then be "picked out" and stereo-typed as problematic. Making a point of befriending those who are different from us is probably the single most important contribution that each of us can offer, in the urgent quest to improve relationships in our global human family, and so safeguard the future of our fragile planet.

What is your own experience?

- What kinds of "foreign" food have you tried? Do you have a preference?
- What is your experience of being with those whose religious and spiritual practices are different from your own?
- What words would you use to categorize the various aspects of your own identity?
- What would it feel like for others to reduce your identity to just one or two words or "labels"?

Try these recipes

- Go out to eat with a friend and try food that you've never tasted before. Before you choose, make a point of speaking with the staff and explain that you want to try something different. Share any concerns you might have (you're vegan, or veggie) and ask for their advice. Get them to tell you about where the recipe comes from and how it's prepared. See what the food or its preparation can tell you that you didn't know about the world we live in.
- Ask the staff whether any particular religious beliefs or practices have contributed to the preparation of your food.
- Find ways of meeting people whose religious or spiritual beliefs are different from your own. Visit their places of worship. Ask them how they see the world and what concerns they have.
- Invite people to come to an "interfaith banquet" where different foods are shared and small groups discuss what it's like to be a minority, or a misunderstood part of a larger society.

The Beginner's Guide to Encountering Religious and Spiritual Difference

There may be times when your life's journey leads you to unexpected places and encounters, when you find yourself thinking: "I've met this really nice person from an entirely different background to my own. What do I need to know?"

Here, fifteen of the major world religions are considered from the point of view of a selection of key criteria. While every person is, of course, an individual and there will be exceptions to every rule, the following may serve us as an initial guide to how not to make a complete fool of ourselves.

	Bahá'í	Buddhist	Chinese Religions	Christian	Hindu
God	One God	No real concept of God	Polytheistic	One God	Basically one God with many manifestations
Prophets etc	Founded by the Báb and Bahá'u'lláh	Founded by Siddhartha Gautama: thr Buddha	Lots of deities	Jesus is the Son of God; prophets in Bible and elsewhere	Hinduism has many sources of inspiration
Texts	The writings of the Báb and Bahá'u'lláh	No single text but the *Dharma* contains Buddha's teaching	Various but the *Tao Te Ching* for Taoists	New Testament and the Bible	The Vedas and sagas like the *Mahābhārata* and the *Ramayana*.
Groups	Just the one	Theravada, Mahayana, and Vajrayana are the major branches	Lots. With Taoism perhaps the best known	Catholics, Protestant, Orthodox and others	Two schools: Vedanta and Yoga
Prayer and meditation	One obligatory daily prayer	Two types of daily meditation: *samatha* and *vipassanā*	Daily	Daily	Daily religious rituals
Food	Vegetarian	No intoxicants	No restrictions	No restrictions	Mostly vegetarian, and never beef

	Bahá'í	Buddhist	Chinese Religions	Christian	Hindu
Alcohol	No	No	Moderation is encouraged	No restrictions	Variable
Activities	No restrictions	No restrictions	No restrictions	No restrictions	No restrictions
Dress Code	No restrictions	No restrictions	No restrictions	No restrictions	No restrictions
Physical contact	No restrictions	No restrictions	No restrictions	No restrictions	Not in public with opposite sex
Dating	No premarital sex	No "sexual misconduct"	No restrictions	No restrictions	Normally organized by the parents
Marriage	No restrictions	No restrictions	No restrictions	No restrictions	Normally organized by the parents
LGBT	Variable	Variable according to culture	No	Variable	No
www.	bahai.org	buddhism facts.net	sacu.org	britannica. com/ christianity	hinduism. ygoy.com

Try Out these Other Recipes

	Humanism	Jainism	Jehovah's Witness	Jewish	Mormon
God	None	No "Creator God"	One God: Jehovah	One God: Yahweh; God is addressed as "Ha Shem"	One God addressed as "Heavenly Father"
Prophets etc	None	The 24 special teachers or Tirthankars who have achieved divinity	Jesus is God's first and only creation, the "only begotten Son"	Various in the Bible ("Old" Testament)	Jesus; Joseph Smith, the Founder
Texts	None	The teachings of the Tirthankars	New Testament and the Bible	Hebrew Bible or "Old" Testament	Book of Mormon and the Bible
Groups	None	Two main groups	Basically just the one	Orthodox, Reform/ Progressive and Liberal	Associated with the Church of Jesus Christ of the Latter-Day Saints
Prayer and meditation	Personal choice	A daily "universal prayer"	Daily	Morning and evening	Daily
Food	No restrictions	Vegetarian	Nothing addictive	Kosher only– and no pork or shell fish	Nothing addictive

	Humanism	Jainism	Jehovah's Witnesses	Jewish	Mormon
Alcohol	No restrictions	No	No	Yes, if it's kosher	No
Activities	No restrictions	No restrictions	No military service, or blood transfusion	No work on the Sabbath (dusk Friday to dusk Saturday)	No restrictions
Dress Code	No restrictions	No restrictions	Modest at all times	Orthodox use hats and wigs	Modest at all times
Physical contact	No restrictions	No restrictions	Not in public with opposite sex	Not in public with opposite sex	Chastity at all times; no sex outside marriage
Dating	No restrictions	No sex outside marriage	Only with other JWs	Best to stick with other Jews	Only with other Mormons
Marriage	No restrictions	No restrictions	Only with other JWs	Best to stick with other Jews	Plural marriage, but only with other Mormons
LGBT	Yes	No	No	Liberal Jews only	Very ambiguous

	Humanism	Jainism	Jehovah's Witnesses	Jewish	Mormon
www.	humanism.org.uk; think humanism.com	jainology.org	jw-media.org	jewfaq.org	mormon.org

	Muslim	Neo-Pagan Religions	Shinto	Sikh	Zoroastrian
God	One God: Allah	Notions of divinity vary widely	No real concept of God	One God addressed as Vāhigurū	One God: Ahura Mazda
Prophets etc	Mohammed	None	The "Sacred Realm" contains gods, spirits and human ancestors	Ten Gurus	Zoroaster or Zarathustra
Texts	Qur'an and Hadith	Many	No core sacred text but various "Histories"	The Gurū Granth Sāhib (or the Ādi Granth) and Dasam Granth	The *Avesta*
Groups	Sunni, Shia (or Shi'ite), Sufis and others	Wiccans, Druids, Pagans, and others	Five main groups	Just the one	Just the one
Prayer and meditation	Five times daily	Celebrations of the cycles and seasons of nature are performed individually and in groups	Periodic and daily purification rituals happen at home or in public shrines	Morning and evening	Worship at home five times daily, facing the light or outside in the open

Food	Halal only– so no pork	Often vegetarian or vegan	No restrictions	Usually vegetarian, & never kosher	Mostly vegetarian
Alcohol	No	No restrictions	No restrictions	No	No
Activities	No gambling	No restrictions	No restrictions	No restrictions	No restrictions
Dress Code	Modest at all times	No restrictions	No restrictions	Modest at all times	Modest at all times
Physical contact	Not in public with opposite sex; no sex outside marriage	No restrictions	Respectful and modest at all times	Not in public with opposite sex	Modest at all times l
Dating	With parental approval only	No restrictions	No restrictions	No sex outside marriage	With parental approval
Marriage	Normally organized by the parents	No restrictions	No restrictions	No restrictions	Ideally with a Zoroastrian
LGBT	No	Yes	Variable according to culture	No	No
www.	islam.com	pagan federation.org	jinjahonto.or .jp	sikhs.org and allaboutsikhs .com	heritagein situte.com

Paying the Bill

Settling the bill

When it's time to settle up after a nice meal out somewhere, who pays the bill? Most societies usually have intricate rules about resolving such matters, but if all else fails it's probably best to agree to share the costs and "go Dutch," especially where the etiquette is unclear, such as on a first date.

But, of course, deciding how to cover the price of one meal is only a relatively minor part of a much bigger picture. For the bill is just the end point in a long chain of transactions, stretching back "who-knows-where" across the world, that links together complex issues of land management, food production, fair trade, transportation, stewardship of money and resources, and global sustainability.

Living within our means

Exercising stewardship and promoting sustainability is not just about being careful with our own money. It's about the lifestyles we live, the ways in which we use the world's natural resources, and the manner of our dealings with the other people and creatures with whom we share the planet, and for whom we have the moral responsibility of caring. So living within "our" means is no longer an issue about our own personal interests and individual well-being, but properly requires a global perspective. And as part of that process we no longer have a choice but to rethink our own expectations and habits of consumption, and consider their impact at the macro level. Living within our means is a deeply spiritual matter!

Spiritual sustainability

For the daily reality, for most of the people of the world, is that there really is "death in the pot." Poor harvests, insufficient food, dirty water, greedy multinational corporations, unfair trade practices, spiraling inflation and debt, and corruption, all contribute to the starvation diet and "less than a dollar a day" existence which is the lot of far too many people. There is no "quick fix," no pain-free solution for the rest of us. Nor does the solution lie in merely saying sorry and in admitting our share of the collective responsibility. People are hungry, homeless, and dying. They can wait no longer.

We need to acknowledge that suffering and evil do often appear to have a life of their own. That it not infrequently seems that, despite all our best intentions, the very institutions, systems, and structures we create are incapable of ensuring the flourishing of people, nations, and the very planet that sustains us all. And while it is usually no one person's "fault" that things are the way they are, it is everyone's responsibility to put things right.

Exploring a political spirituality of relationality

What's required is a spirituality that willingly embraces action. A spirituality that is eager to scrutinize and challenge "structural sin" – those mechanisms of exclusion and disciplines of power than keep the world order as it is. And if we choose to call ourselves spiritual people, then we really have no option but to engage with the issues.

Today, as never before, we must commit ourselves to doing our utmost to stand up for what is right, to speak out, and to fight for a just and inclusive global society, with a fair distribution of – and access to – food, wealth, and power *for all the people of the world.*

Creative spirituality seeks to connect personal responsibility with a commitment to action for justice, peace, and flourishing for all people and for our planet. Whatever form it takes, "good" spirituality is ultimately "political," because it's about recognizing that *relationality* is at the heart of human existence and human values. That all the people involved in the cultivation, manufacture, or processing of everything we consume are, in a very real sense, *as much our concern as if they were guests at our own table.* And though we may delegate this responsibility to governments and institutions, it is still very much our duty to diligently hold these agencies and systems to account. The hard reality is that accountability for "paying the bill" is ultimately everyone's concern.

What is your own experience?

- How do you try to ensure that you're living within your personal means?
- How do you distinguish between your needs and your desires?
- What are your honest expectations about the quality of your own future lifestyle?
- How do these expectations relate to your spiritual practices?
- To what extent are your own spiritual practices relational?

Try these recipes

- Next time you prepare a meal at home, or go shopping for food, take time to check the labels for the sources of your food. Who produces it? Where has it come from? Use the

internet to trace the food back "to its roots." Try to find the
original producer, and the conditions under which their
employees work and live. Look out for the kinds of
compromise we all have to make. Is it preferable to have
locally grown food with reduced transport costs, but
where workers earn more? Or better to have the food
grown overseas, more cheaply, and fairly traded, but with
much greater transports costs and carbon emissions? How
do you see the issues? What compromises are you happy
to make?

- Sit down alone, and then with a group of friends from
  different religious or spiritual backgrounds, and try to
  identify the "markers" – the values and practices – that
  inform your own stewardship. What can you learn from
  other people?

- Using the material about being "introvert" and "extrovert"
  (see "Spirituality and Personality"), try to identify ways in
  which to explore, to a greater extent than before, how you
  might develop personal spiritual practices that are
  oriented towards, or expressed through, other people or
  through an awareness of our fundamental interdependence
  and connectedness to others.

- What might you do to show solidarity with the people,
  either locally or internationally, who are exploited or
  marginalized by our economic systems?

First Aid, Help, and Hygiene

Living to eat – or eating to live?

Over the last few years the world's attention has periodically been drawn to the story of Mr. Prahlad Jani, an Indian "fakir" or holy man, who has apparently not eaten or drunk for most of his seventy years of life and has suffered no ill effects. While the majority of people are, at best, able to go a few weeks without food, and only a few days without water, this case seems baffling. Is it a simple hoax, as some claim, or is he actually managing to survive and be healthy on "spiritual energy" alone? This would have very interesting spin-offs if it proves to be the case. But time alone will tell.

The French dramatist Molière puts the dilemma of our relationship with food in a different way when he asks whether we live to eat, or eat to live. Think about it for a moment!

Good food delights the soul, and eating it – alone or with others – can play a significant role in many people's spiritual lives. But while even simple fare is a necessary and unremarkable part of our ordinary daily existence, food is also a highly problematic and painful issue for more people than we ever probably imagine.

Eating conditions

For large numbers of us will suffer at some point in our lives with eating disorders such as Bulimia nervosa and Anorexia nervosa, from gastrointestinal problems, such as Crohn's disease, as well as from a wide range of food intolerances and allergies; to say nothing of obesity. While the origins of these health complaints are often unclear and may arise from a mixture of social, biological, or psychological factors, it's important to remember that there is no value or reason for anyone to suffer in silence. Help is available if we have any concerns or fears, and resources exist to address these and help manage the conditions. As with all health issues the first port of call is always our medical practitioner, clinic, or counselor. And rather than being tempted to follow the advice of dubious internet sites and "support" groups, good on-line resources can be found via the British Association for Counselling and Psychotherapy (www.bacp.co.uk) and the American Counseling Association (www.counseling.org).

Spiritual dysfunction and crisis

Yet a parallel set of problems will arise, sooner or later, with those of us trying to understand, manage, and develop our spiritual "dietary requirements" or explore a new "regime" for our souls.

For, just as poor nutrition can impact psychologically and spiritually, so poor spiritual nourishment can lead to problems with our physical and mental well-being. And, it goes without saying that, from time to time, we will all discover "intolerances" or things that just don't suit who we are; to say nothing of "allergic" reactions to certain spiritual practices that we might try. Or else there will be occasions when a new "diet" or discipline doesn't appear to work, or even seems to produce contrary results, or when we feel despondent and some "First Aid" or "TLC" is needed.

Resources

Just as there are medically trained personnel and skilled counselors for the whole spectrum of eating conditions, so there are also counselors and therapists who are happy to deal with existential and spiritual issues.

But whether or not we would choose to describe ourselves as "religious," the sheer quantity of spiritual wisdom and practical experience that the religious traditions have is certainly worth exploring. A vast range of resources exists – and the best of it is free!

There are good and wise clergy, chaplains, and campus ministers from all the world religions, as well as thousands of places of worship to visit and experience. As we have seen, many faith-based practitioners offer "spiritual direction" in one form or another, and such people are very certainly worth engaging in conversation. Exploring your spiritual path is often more interesting and worthwhile with a guide or else in the company of others.

Hygiene matters

The spiritual equivalents of common sense kitchen hygiene also have to be followed when it comes to soul nurture. Chief amongst these is honesty: the spiritual equivalent of cleanliness. There is no point in self deception. Being true to ourselves is crucial at all times. Next comes the use of authentic and wholesome ingredients. There is much bad religion "out there," to say nothing of unscrupulous practitioners wanting to make a quick buck. Authenticity and wholesomeness can usually be recognized by the transparency of individuals, and by the openness and gentleness with which they operate. Any hints of trying to control, intimidate, deceive, or belittle should trigger alarm bells. If you have any concerns with an individual, group, or practice, then seek advice immediately from someone you trust. A *bona fide* religious or spiritual practitioner will never be offended if you ask endless questions, disagree vehemently, and then choose never to go back!

Finally, just as everything we consume needs to be properly cooked or prepared to avoid ill effects, so we must all learn the ancient (and at times frustrating!) art of patience. In the same way that there is a necessary waiting period while food is cooked, if it's to be nutritionally beneficial, *so it takes time* for the transformation of our souls. Often a whole life time: which, however, is precisely the time available to us all! So don't rush things. Pace yourself. Be gentle with yourself. And your patience will always be rewarded.

What is your own experience?

- What part does food play in your own life, daily routines, and spiritual disciplines?
- How does what you eat impact on the person you are?
- What spiritual practices have you tried that had a negative effect on you? What did you do?

Try these recipes

- Take time to sit and talk with someone from a religious or spiritual tradition that is familiar to you, or that you think you know. Ask them the questions that matter to you.
- Take time to sit and talk with someone from a religious or spiritual tradition that is outside your own experience. Ask them the questions that matter to you.
- What advice, hints, or guidance would you offer to other soul travelers who are concerned about their own spiritual diet?

SHARE WITH OTHERS +++

Recipes for Sharing

Commandments and such like

Religions and spiritual traditions are full of "Advice." But there is "Advice" and "advice." The world's great religious ethical codes are usually set out in the form of eternally valid truths revealed "from on high" and often literally "set in stone," or dictated by the mouth or mind of God. So the Jewish scriptures record six hundred and thirteen "mitzvot" or commandments. Christianity has the "Decalogue," or "Ten Commandments," which it shares with Judaism. Islam has its "Five Pillars," Hinduism its "Five Principles and Ten Commandments," Sikhism its "Khalsa" and the teaching of the Ten Gurus. Often the numbers five and ten are significant – no doubt connected with the number of fingers on our hands, so as to facilitate memorization. But even in this post-modern "digital" age we can find the traditional alive and well in the form of the "Ten Commandments of Computer Ethics" of the Computer Ethics Institute, Washington DC!

Now there is no doubt that these ethical codes have been spectacularly important in shaping the world as we know it. And while there is, in the West, a certain suspicion of the *uncritical* valuing of "divinely revealed truth" – a suspicion that is frequently justified whenever we see its misuse to subjugate women, minorities, and "outsiders" – yet there is a sense in which the function and relevance of such truth may be not waning, but merely changing.

Grit in the oyster

One of the things that some Christians, and others, often misunderstand is why Jesus said he wasn't concerned with getting rid of the Jewish commandments or "Law" (Matthew 5:17-18). One of the reasons for this misunderstanding is that people forget that

Jesus was – and remained – faithfully Jewish. The other is because they fail to see that so much of his role as a prophet – like the great prophets of Israel before him – was bound up with his *critical stance* towards the interpretation and application of the Law.

It's as though the Law functioned as the creative spur against which he reacted, and which empowered and directed his life's work. Just like the grain of sand or grit that gets sucked into an oyster shell. While its presence provokes the oyster into producing protective "saliva," the end result is, quite literally, a pearl of great price!

So while we may find ourselves with a somewhat – or even a more than somewhat – *uncomfortable or dismissive* attitude towards the historic religious codes, it may likely be that they can still serve to inform or shape our own attitudes and religious or spiritual practices. Even only in so far as we react against them.

Offering food and drink for other hungry soul travelers

The question then remains as to how we would now articulate our own "pearls of great price." We may choose to talk of our own ten – or nineteen, twenty-seven, fifty-five and three-quarters, or ninety-one and a half – commandments. (Somehow odd numbers and fractions seem more "true-to-life" than numbers that are "whole" or "complete"!) Or whether we would prefer, instead, to talk of models to be explored and later superceded, or recipes to be tested and improved by trial and error and modified according to individual tastes.

We may feel that these are immensely private matters. Or we may want to shy away from offering "advice" of any sort. But given all that we have discovered about the fundamental connection between personal spirituality, human interdependence, and global responsibility, perhaps we might just consider that the world could be a better place for everyone if we dared ourselves to share the fragments of wisdom and insight that we have collected on our own journeys?

Because it's worth it

It's time now for you to go solo. A cookery book of any sort can only teach so much, and sooner or later there's really no substitute for creative experimentation on our own. Sure, the odd disaster will always happen, but that's nothing that can't now be coped with. The journey's the thing; and it's now time to set off again.

What's your own experience?

Make a list of all the wise recipes that you have discovered, begged, borrowed, stolen, or been given. Here are a few for starters. The rest is for you to start completing.

- Never doubt you are unique and amazing
- Keep picking yourself up and starting again
- Do as little harm as you can
- Remember your responsibilities

Try this final recipe

- Make your own "rule of life." Let it be a succinct description of all that you like and value, all that you aspire to be, and all that you would like to offer to the world. Practice it daily. Review it periodically. Be gentle with yourself, but remain determined to be the difference that you would like to see in the world.

Exercises for Setting off Again

Exercise Number One

You make now like to give your own responses to the following questions. Remember the value of honesty, authenticity, wholesomeness, and patience.

1 *What responses do you have and what connections do you make on seeing a glorious sunset?*
2 *What's really important to you at this stage of your life?*
3 *What makes you really fulfilled?*
4 *How do you handle times of darkness, despondency, and depression?*
5 *What do you feel about your body?*
6 *How would you describe your spirituality in one sentence, phrase, or image?*
7 *What do relationships mean to you?*
8 *What place does silence have in your life?*
9 *How do you link spirituality and action?*
10 *What makes you feel connected to the rest of humanity and creation?*
11 *How do you understand the idea of personal ambition?*
12 *How would you like to be remembered?*

Once again there are no scores. Whatever you've written is right for you at this moment in your life!

Exercise Number Two

Make a list of all the "big questions" that fascinate you. Let these be food for your journey!

Exercise Number Three

Devise ways for ensuring you continue to flourish spiritually, and for sharing what you have learned with those around you.

Afterword

Setting out on the road to independent living is a time of discontinuity and disruption for the majority of young people, as well as an exciting adventure. Indeed, it's perhaps the last great rite of passage in our secular society. There is evidence that, for some young people, joining a campus faith group or student society serves as a kind of transition stage between the security of the family home and values, and the self-responsibility of independent living and thinking.[7] But such groups, while open to everyone (and indeed often actively seeking "converts"), generally fail to attract the majority of students who have little or no interest in religion *per se*.

The hope of this book is to find a way of enabling this majority of students and young people to interact with and explore an area of life that is, to my mind, both of critical importance to personal, social, and global flourishing, and also hugely neglected. That's to say the area of "the spiritual."

The spiritual – spirituality – is a phenomenon that is of considerable interest today. While, for some people, their spirituality may include a religious dimension, discipline, or allegiance, many people actually experience "the spiritual dimension," and practice their spirituality, quite separately and distinctly from the religious realm. Many others are not even aware that they have a spiritual dimension and are intrigued to discover and explore it.

The assumption of this book – supported by detailed research from many quarters[8] – is that everyone has a spiritual dimension. While, for some, the terms "spiritual" and "spirituality" are problematic because they appear to be too closely related to the idea of religion, there is no satisfactory or commonly accepted alternative.

It is perhaps better simply to accept that "spirituality" is a highly subjective term that refers to that collage of disciplines and practices, and to those "deepest values and meanings, by which people seek to live."[9] And that this collage serves to enable mature self-realization, as part of the on-going project of striving for the flourishing of the whole human family and the health of our global ecosystem. It also serves as part of our response to that sense of "otherness" that we experience within ourselves, in our daily living, and in our relationships with other people and our environment. That "otherness" which some may name as "God."

But faith groups – of whatever "flavor" – have not done people any favors by the way in which they have tended to dress up the language of the spiritual. I have often felt that the churches, for instance, have effectively deprived people of accessible and meaningful language to articulate their own spiritual experience, by removing the "spiritual" from daily life into the realm of the "sacred," and then to encase it within theological jargon or dogma. And I hear similar things from young members of other faith groups too.

Nor is it just the "faith" communities. A while back I held

some seminars on prayer and spirituality with a number of Humanists, where most of those present seemed to be prevented from naming certain aspects of their experience of life as "spiritual" by the dogma of their disbelief in God. A smaller number was, however, intrigued to think what "Humanist spirituality" might look like, and was keen to explore it!

One of the tactics that all of these groups – the religious and the non-religious alike – tend to employ, is to attempt to claim for themselves all rights to "name" the "spiritual." They say: "ah well. It all depends on what you mean by *spiritual*." As if they had sole rights to define and interpret the term. As though only their version of "spirituality" were the correct one.

That's not to say that the great world religions don't have immense experience and resources – spiritual treasures – to offer people. They do! But a large part of the problem is that they have consistently failed to find the most effective ways of doing so. They don't listen to people!

The experience seems all too often to have been, that if you want to talk about spirituality to a representative member of a faith community – pastor, priest, rabbi, imam – they fail to understand. Or else they are totally incapable of thinking outside the box of their own theological or religious tradition and language, in order to begin the conversation where people actually are, and with the questions that people are actually asking.

So this book is an attempt to address some of the basic issues. It doesn't assume any religious adherence or experience on the part of the reader, but it does try to look at some common themes in spirituality as might be encountered in ordinary daily living in the secular West.

It imitates the form of a cookery book and offers "spiritual recipes" to nourish the "inner" personal, and "outer" social, situation of young people stepping out independently into the world for the first time, in the hope that they will learn to flourish, and not be withered and waste away. It's also meant to be enjoyably creative. Just like my own cooking!

It's written by an Anglican priest who works as a chaplain across three higher education institutions in Manchester, UK. While I spend some of my time each week on "Christian matters," and a good deal working with colleagues from the other world religions, much more of my time is spent with students of no particular faith as they seek to explore ideas, feelings, and situations that matter to them. The questions they have posed, and the dilemmas they have faced are, in large part, responsible for shaping the content of this book

In particular I am indebted to the students of St Anselm Hall of the University of Manchester who, over the past seven years, have never ceased to ask insightful questions of me. I am hugely grateful to David Masters and Stuart Robb who have read the whole text, and offered creative and insightful comments on every draft – though the responsibility for the contents remains entirely mine. I would like to thank Laura Betson, Stephen Canning, and Hannah Pauly, for their feedback on individual sections, and John Walker for his energizing enthusiasm for my original ideas for the book, one hot summer in France.

In particular I want to express my deep appreciation to Fiona for her wonderful illustrations that have brought visible depth to my words. Fiona trained at the Norwich School of Art, UK, and is currently studying for an MA in London. Her pictures are a hand drawn collage of coloured pencil and felt tip pen. For more information, or just to say hello, please go to www.pinkpaper-circus.com.

Then I want to thank my daughter Hannah for her dancing and, most especially, to my wife Jayne Prestwood who has taught me more about the joys of life that anyone else has ever managed to do. It is to her that I dedicate this book.

Terry Biddington
The Feast of the Holy Spirit 2010

Endnotes

1 Thomas Moore, *Care of the Soul*, London: Piatkus, 1992, p.x.
2 *Care of the Soul*, p.ix.
3 Irenaeus of Lyons, *Against Heresies*, Book Four, Chapter 20, www.ccel.org.
4 From his poem "Leisure," in *Songs Of Joy and Others* www.bliolife.com/opensource.
5 *As You Like It*, Act II, Scene VII.
6 From his poem "Bishop Blougram's Apology," line 395.
7 See Edward Dutton, *Meeting Jesus at University. Rites of Passage and Student Experience*, London: Ashgate, 2008, *passim*.
8 Paul Heelas and Linda Woodhead, *The Spiritual Revolution: Why Religion is Giving Way to Spirituality*, Oxford: Blackwell, 2005, *passim*.
9 Philip Sheldrake, *A Brief History of Spirituality*, Oxford: Blackwell, 2007, p.1.

Circle Books

Circle is a symbol of infinity and unity. It's part of a growing list of imprints, including o-books.net and zero-books.net.

Circle Books aims to publish books in Christian spirituality that are fresh, accessible, and stimulating.

Our books are available in all good English language bookstores worldwide. If you can't find the book on the shelves, then ask your bookstore to order it for you, quoting the ISBN and title. Or, you can order online—all major online retail sites carry our titles.

To see our list of titles, please view www.Circle-Books.com, growing by 80 titles per year.

Authors can learn more about our proposal process by going to our website and clicking on Your Company > Submissions.

We define Christian spirituality as the relationship between the self and its sense of the transcendent or sacred, which issues in literary and artistic expression, community, social activism, and practices. A wide range of disciplines within the field of religious studies can be called upon, including history, narrative studies, philosophy, theology, sociology, and psychology. Interfaith in approach, Circle Books fosters creative dialogue with non-Christian traditions.

And tune into MySpiritRadio.com for our book review radio show, hosted by June-Elleni Laine, where you can listen to authors discussing their books.

MySpiritRadio